Black White Green Red

Educational Policy, Planning, and Theory
Series Editor: Don Adams, University of Pittsburgh

Black White Green Red
The Politics of Education in Ethnic America

David Bresnick
Seymour Lachman
Murray Polner

Longman

New York and London

BLACK/WHITE/GREEN/RED
The Politics of Education in Ethnic America

Longman Inc., New York
Associated companies, branches, and representatives
throughout the world.

Developmental Editor: Edward Artinian
Editorial and Design Supervisor: Linda Salmonson
Design: Pencils Portfolio, Inc.
Manufacturing and Production Supervisor: Louis Gaber
Composition: Fuller Typesetting of Lancaster
Printing and Binding: The Murray Printing Company

Library of Congress Cataloging in Publication Data

Bresnick, David.
  Black/white/green/red.

  (Educational policy, planning, and theory)
  Bibliography: p.
  Includes index.
    1. Minorities—Education—United States.
2. Politics and education. I. Lachman, Seymour,
joint author. II. Polner, Murray, joint author.
III. Title.
LC3731.P64   370.19'342'0973   77–18306
ISBN 0–582–28042–7

Manufactured in the United States of America

Contents

Introduction   vii

Chapter 1 What It's All About   1

Chapter 2 The End of Ocean Hill–Brownsville   16

Chapter 3 Beating the Bureaucracy   40

Chapter 4 Changing the Way Education Is   66

Chapter 5 Struggling for Student Rights   90

Chapter 6 Integration, Busing, and Community
Control Revisited   117

Conclusions   150

Selected Bibliography   159

Index   162

Introduction

This is the story of the large city school systems of this country during the late 1960s and the early 1970s. Black and Hispanic groups, representing the emerging new ethnic groups in the cities, demanded community control. During that time the three authors of this book were working for the New York City Board of Education.

Seymour Lachman was a new member (and later president) of the Board of Education. Murray Polner and David Bresnick were initially his staff aides. Afterward Polner became executive assistant to the first chancellor of schools, and Bresnick later directed a program of management assistance to the new community school boards.

Many of the people we met there must have felt a twinge of conscience from time to time: What had all the maneuvering and all the posturing to do with a single child in any one classroom? Very early in his tenure, in a fit of pique, the New York City Schools Chancellor Harvey Scribner lashed out against adults caught up in such power plays. They cared only for themselves, he said with genuine anger, and not one whit for students. John Lindsay had once said much the same when he first took office as mayor and denounced the "power brokers" in the city.

But when had it been otherwise? The men and women who competed daily in the bruising setting of school politics, often representing in one way or another specific interest groups, were in the business of personal or group gain and power. No single group dominated. Blocs were themselves divided. Few could advance proposals but many could object. And in terms of power, in day-to-day decisions, it was who counted at the moment, what the stakes were, and who brought the most pressure. For the Board of Education, too, often reacted to events, especially during its first years when the vision of chaos and verbal license from its petitioners threatened to overwhelm it. Six million dollars for security guards were "found" after a vitriolic demonstration by a city councilman. After the state comptroller released—as he so often did—charges of fiscal errors, only then would the Board make inquiries. The Board often acted when its back was against the wall, when civil wars erupted in the school districts, and critics publicly pressed their views.

For many, including some of the highest officials at central headquarters, the great prizes were not teaching children to read, compute competently, or develop critical thinking, but good salaries, extravagant pensions, patronage, and influence. For some few it meant limousines, chauffeurs, television interviews, press headlines, and even instant recognition. It was heady stuff and more than some could resist.

This book is about municipal unions and the civil service, about blacks and Hispanics and white ethnics, about parents and politicians and journalists, the schools chancellor, and the five lay Board members. It also considers the movements for educational change then so nationally popular. What was meant by change? Toward what ends did it move? What was the role of the chancellor and the Board and their staffs in advancing or retarding its progress? Where did the bureaucracy at central headquarters—110 Livingston Street —play its role? The community school boards? The press? The tax-exempt foundations? The unions? The civic associations? The parent groups, both elite and popular? Where, indeed, did all of them fit? Most significantly, to what extent did racial and ethnic concerns affect the outcomes? In short, who applied what strength for what purposes?

We think the answers to many of these questions, while far from definitive, will surprise a good many readers, essentially dependent on the instant news of the media. Holding a morning paper that featured the "inside" story on a school issue, one Board member turned to another in early 1973 and asked, "Who the hell knows what the truth is?"

For one of the difficulties in pursuing the dynamics and process of instituting school reforms was that reformers, real or rhetorical, sweeping or one-step-at-a-time, were inundated with hawkers of new dogmas and panaceas, maddeningly unclarified, unchallenged, and undocumented. One of the reformers bragged publicly, "We have the answers already, you have only to reach out for them." Time and again, the New Hucksters were dared to prove their premises and test their results, yet not one offered to do so. It was evident that the instructional processes in this country's big city public schools had shown very little improvement during the 1960s. Reading, mathematics, thinking logically, and writing clearly remained, for too many students, elusive goals. Nonetheless, many sincere critics remained convinced that solutions were at hand, if only some ill-defined alterations, some piece of technology, some variation in instruction, some new faces, some added freedoms, or some more money were introduced.

In the end all this contributed to the mad-hatter's world in which we all worked. For schools—public schools, at least— were the soft underbelly of American urban society, the battleground, and safety valve for frustrations. The most wealthy and powerful in the city rarely sent their children to them and, except for occasional pontification, permitted the schools to become punching bags. Without the elite's support and interest, and without the support of the vast majority of New York's citizens who do not have any children in the public schools, power could only be limited and fragmented, and the schools, and especially inner-city schools, would continue to stagnate.

Although this book concerns itself with school politics

throughout the country, it draws heavily on in-depth case studies of New York City. Where possible, however, we have referred to more general studies and the experience of other cities. As we worked through the available material, we often found that it raised more questions than it answered. We hope this book is as suggestive for our readers.

What It's All About

Ocean Hill–Brownsville and Canarsie are two Brooklyn neighborhoods. Ocean Hill–Brownsville, the scene from 1966 to 1968 of a struggle for community control, is almost entirely black and Puerto Rican. Canarsie is overwhelmingly white, yet in 1973 and 1974 it, too, witnessed a struggle for community control.

These ethnic conflicts are not unlike those which have pervaded New York City politics since the mid-nineteenth century. The winter of 1968 was the scene of perhaps the most sustained ethnic conflict in the city's history. Many Jews and blacks, who only a few years before had been sitting-in together in the cause of integration in the South, were now at each others' throats. A decade after the 1968 teachers' strike, one recalls the names of Rhody McCoy and John Lindsay, who with Albert Shanker made national headlines. Rhody McCoy, a veteran of twenty years in the New York City school system, was the black unit administrator of Ocean Hill–Brownsville, the first district created to

demonstrate the feasibility of community control. Albert
Shanker remains the president of the United Federation of
Teachers, the strongest teachers' local in the country (and
has since also become the president of the American
Federation of Teachers). Mayor John Lindsay attempted to
mediate between them and their constituencies, sometimes
forgetting that he represented New York's oldest and most
potent ethnic group. To a national television audience, Albert
Shanker and Rhody McCoy symbolized the conflict between
Jews and blacks, with John Lindsay, the WASP mayor,
caught in between, condemned by both sides.

During the late sixties, the struggle of the new ethnic
groups, the blacks and Hispanics, centered on the public
schools. The demands for "black and Hispanic power"
fueled the movement for community control and for direct
authority over decision making in the schools.

From the perspective of almost a decade, that conflict is
seen to have been much more deeply rooted than it appeared
at the time. Its manifestations within the educational
bureaucracy were an early warning of trouble in other areas.
Tension over jobs in the construction industry and the
uniformed services was yet to come. Turmoil over low-income
public housing located in middle-class areas was still
ahead. But the schools were more vulnerable to protest and
pressure. Black and Hispanic dissatisfaction with the
educational bureaucracy and what was happening to their
young in the schoolroom led to bitter frustration. The failure
of the American educational system to provide rapid social
mobility or even educational success for black and Hispanic
children was, they reasoned, proof that it was, indeed, only
another American myth that education provided an upward
path for their children.

Community control, the watchword of the newly activated
black and Hispanic groups, came as a shock to many of
the participants in the civil rights movement, for it seemed to

fly in the face of earlier commitments to racial "integration."
Many adherents of integration saw it as a strategy for
assimilation, leaving behind the inferior status associated
with segregation. They subscribed to the beliefs articulated
by a prominent social scientist, Amos Hawley, in the
mid-1940s: "Redistribution of a minority group in the same
territorial pattern as that of the majority groups results in
a dissipation of subordinate status and an assimilation of the
subjugated group into the social structure."

Antagonism between integration and separatist strategies
was perhaps most clearly juxtaposed in the formation of
the demonstration district around Intermediate School 201 in
Harlem. During the summer of 1966, parent groups, led by
the Harlem Parents Council, which had advocated the
integration of IS 201 by bringing in white students, realized
that the Board of Education was unable to fulfill its promise.
Drawing upon theoreticians Richard Cloward and Preston
Wilcox, these groups made a complete turnabout to advocate
community control for IS 201.

Community control represented a departure from preceding
trends and a turning away from integration. Activists within
the black and Hispanic communities no longer favored
bringing their children together with white children. Rather,
they sought to gain control over their own school systems.
Community control questioned the ability of the administration
and teachers to educate youngsters. Its adherents questioned
the ability of white supervisors and teachers to provide
adequate instruction and role models for black and Hispanic
youngsters. Such questions reinforced the demand for the
employment in the schools of more members of the new
ethnic groups.

Although the dichotomy between integration and
segregation seemed particularly incongruous at the time,
a more detached look at ethnic politics in the larger cities of
the United States might have softened that inconsistency.

For, as each new group reached the large American urban centers, its members had been faced with a similar dilemma: How could they survive and prosper in the larger society, which was dominated by other ethnic groups, where advancement was regulated by a variety of informal mechanisms for social and economic mobility?

Education had been a critical dimension in this quest of immigrants for the better life. It was a central aspect of the dream of equal opportunity based upon individual merit. Anyone could attend public school and those with superior ability could qualify for educational and, later, professional rewards. Education also represented the most immediate contact of new ethnic groups with American institutions. This initial contact was particularly significant, since it presented anew the classic conflict between assimilation and ethnic assertiveness. While offering the prospect of social mobility, the schools demanded compliance with the values of the dominant society.

A general pattern emerged. As new ethnic groups became better established, their interest in the educational bureaucracy expanded. Education represented a source of jobs and contracts for equipment, supplies, and evalutions. Thus, educational politics was part of the larger game of ethnic politics. Individuals and their groups sought to influence decisions made by the educational bureaucracy. They operated within the existing political system, which, in New York City and many other large cities, depended to a large extent on ethnic organization.

In education, ethnic studies were the key manifestation of a trend toward greater group awareness. Just as colleges began introducing departments of black and Hispanic studies, demands arose for greater attention to ethnic history and heritage in the lower schools. Black culture became a watchword in many circles, and the effort of the schools to make students aware of their past reached substantial proportions. To some it seemed that the schools had gone overboard and were verging on a reversal of their traditional role of assimilating hyphenated groups into the American melting pot and were stressing the differences that separated and divided Americans, instead.

To some, ethnic awareness extended to more traditional areas of education. New methods of instruction, especially adapted to the ethnic background of the new ethnic groups, were sought.

The demand for ethnically specific curricula led to demands for greater ethnic representation in teaching and supervisory positions. Black and Hispanic children, or so the argument ran, needed black and Hispanic teachers because they were more "sensitive" to the children's specific language and cultural needs. The children needed adults from their own ethnic groups to serve as role models. This insistence on greater recognition of their own ethnic identity led inevitably to the demand for greater ethnic representation in the educational bureaucracy.

During the late 1960s, black and Hispanic groups drew upon the American belief in ethnic assertion as a route to social mobility. Finding their private resources inadequate and the barriers in the private sector overwhelming, they seized upon the increasing role of government largesse to demand control of government resources. In a prophetic statement made before the development of the community action programs and the black power movement of the mid-sixties, Congressman Adam Clayton Powell argued that, since blacks were 21 percent of the Democratic party enrollment in Manhattan, they should get 20 percent of the jobs in New York City. Community control gained a peculiar force of its own and in the process incurred the wrath of white ethnic groups, who themselves had used governmental largesse to promote their own interests. Just as the symbolic value of community control slogans mobilized the black and

Hispanic communities to demand government jobs, this explicit demand for governmental intervention in behalf of black and Hispanic groups gave rise to the demand by other groups to remove ethnic politics from job considerations. The new ethnic symbolism and its concomitant mobilization and countermobilization form an important part of the background of the new ethnic politics of the 1970s.

Demands for jobs were encouraged by the community action programs and the community corporations. They showed how blacks and Hispanics, in control of local poverty funds, could use those funds to provide jobs for members of their own ethnic groups. Where, on a city-wide basis, the other ethnic groups in the city seemed to be in control, on a local level, particularly in the ghetto areas of Harlem and Bedford-Stuyvesant, it was clear that boards of local citizens would inevitably represent the locally dominant ethnic groups.

In hoping to use government funds in the form of jobs and perquisites, such as welfare and business contracts, to bolster the fortunes of members of their own ethnic groups, the blacks and Hispanics were following an approved pattern of American immigrant behavior. Accounts of how ethnic groups gained access to the resources of local government through the development of fraternal and religious organizations and control of local party mechanisms are well known in social science literature and are clearly associated with accounts of the party machine.

The quest of new ethnic groups depended ultimately on access to jobs. In a classic study of the assimilation of urban ethnic groups in America, the sociologist Stanley Lieberson found that, generally, the longer their members resided in the United States, the greater the similarity of their job structure to that of the prevailing Anglo-Saxon group. The major exception to this generalization was the black group, which seemed to be losing ground. The peculiar pattern of blacks' difficulty in gaining access to jobs and higher status has been documented in a number of professions including teaching. Daniel P. Moynihan and Nathan Glazer, in *Beyond the Melting Pot,* pointed out that the only areas of white-collar employment in which there were really large numbers of blacks were the government agencies. In attempting to provide an explanation for this phenomenon, Bennett Harrison, in *Education, Training and the Urban Ghetto,* posits the existence of a dual labor market, which excludes blacks from jobs open to whites. In attaining jobs in public bureaucracies, he argues, new ethnic groups have had to replace previous ethnic groups and have encountered severe obstacles.

Studies of ethnic succession in large city bureaucracies have been rare. The most comprehensive study examines succession in New Haven among individuals of Italian descent; Jerome Meyers studied their penetration of four levels of government jobs. Defining a "quota fulfillment index" as the ratio of jobs attained by an ethnic group to the number of jobs reflecting its proportion in the population, Meyers argued that the time lag between attainment of sizable minority status and representation in the bureaucracy was prolonged. He found that penetration of the elective sphere preceded massive penetration of other sectors, substantiating the argument that ethnic groups must gain political power to secure entry into the civil service system.

Theodore Lowi, in his study of ethnic succession among the higher appointive offices of the civil service of New York City, *At the Pleasure of the Mayor,* wrote: "Decisions on nominations and appointments in New York City have always been weighted heavily with ethnic and religious considerations."

Indeed, the combination of native-American Protestant and Irish Catholic ethnic groups that ran New York City through the 1920s maintained its domination of appointive offices so well that until 1930, 60 to 70 percent of all cabinet appointments and 80 to 85 percent of lesser appointments were dominated by them. Lowi believes the party machinery tended to work against the entry of new minorities into appointive positions.

The distribution of appointments did not respond steadily to the movement of new minorities into politics. The rate of entry into the cabinet of the three most significant new groups was governed largely by the minority party— Republican-Fusion Mayors Seth Low, John Mitchel, and Fiorello La Guardia. Each of these mayors appointed substantially larger numbers of Jewish, Italian, and black representatives than had their Democratic predecessors.

But these new minorities did not achieve representation in places of power until long after they had attained considerable numbers in the population and electorate. Even though the Irish had achieved considerable presence in New York City by 1850, as late as 1860 Boss Tweed still represented the Scotch and Scotch-Irish. The Jews and Italians who arrived at the turn of the century did not assume power until the La Guardia regime, between 1933 and 1945.

By the 1960s, part of the appeal of "community control" was the feeling that it provided a strategy—based upon the creation of small governmental units—for achieving more rapid access to power for black and Hispanic populations. Such access, it was believed, could be clearly demonstrated in terms of ethnic representation among teachers within the educational bureaucracy. This line of reasoning was derived from traditional politics, in which ward systems and local elections were associated with greater power for new ethnic groups.

Ethnic politics in America has been closely linked to the party machine. The party machine came to dominate big city politics toward the end of the nineteenth century, and has continued to prosper and remain powerful in many parts of the country. Although the machines appeared to predate the influx of large Irish populations to the big cities, they have become associated with the rise of this first great new ethnic group in nineteenth-century America. Moynihan and Glazer, for example, argue that the rise of the political machine in America is associated with the style of life brought with the Irish to their new country.

The political machines operated as exchange mechanisms. In return for votes and monetary support, party favors were dispensed, including access to governmental decisions, especially those affecting the awards of contracts and jobs. Operating through local representatives disparagingly referred to as "ward heelers," political machines developed political support and controlled access to government jobs.

The ward heeler's role depended upon the existence of local governmental units, or wards, within which governmental decisions were made. Policemen and teachers, for example, were hired at the ward level, often subject to the consent of the ward heeler. When the reform movements of the late nineteenth and early twentieth century attacked the party machine and the ward system of patronage, a prominent part of the attack focused on the buying of votes of poor immigrants through the spreading of governmental largesse. Many revisionist urban historians have since interpreted that reform movement as an attempt of the displaced elites to regain control—or at least to limit the gains of the new ethnic groups, which had attained power in the cities. An integral part of the reform strategy was replacing ward systems with city-wide elections. In fact, the notoriety of the ward system and its connection with new ethnic-group success stems in large part from the attacks upon it launched by the reformers of the late nineteenth and early twentieth century. This criticism of ethnic politics reinforced the viewpoint that systems of local politics increased the power of ethnic groups newly arising to power.

During the period of Lyndon B. Johnson's "Great Society," one of the central issues raised by the War on Poverty was the extent to which black and Puerto Rican "minorities" might be afforded social mobility through increased access to public sector jobs. While minority criticisms of urban "inner-city" services took a variety of forms, including the assertion that black and Spanish-speaking teachers were needed to "better relate" to the black and Spanish-speaking children, a more important element of this criticism was the attempt to bring members of these groups into public service jobs.

A major rationale for the creation of the community action agencies was to provide employment for groups that found it difficult to compete within the existing local hiring systems. Just as earlier ethnic groups had captured parts of city bureaucracies, the black and Spanish-speaking groups attempted to use the community corporations and the community development agencies as a means of directing their own group members into jobs. The lack of success of these efforts is attributable, at least in part, to the failure of the architects of the community action agencies to construct bridges, which would allow crossovers from community action to other city agencies, and the failure to institutionalize the provisional working titles into civil service titles, with attendant job protection and advancement opportunities. Similarly, one of the reasons for the retrenchment in the community action programs was the opposition of existing political and ethnic groups that found their own positions threatened.

The demand of "maximum feasible participation" in the poverty program and the creation of Title I advisory boards, under the Elementary and Secondary Education Act of 1965, involved local people, reflecting the predominant community

ethnic mix in the determinations of policy. These prerogatives
included the determination of staffing requirements and led
to the growth of dependent groups of employed individuals,
in many cases without civil service protection, who found
that political involvement held the best chance of job
continuity. The attention of Title I advisory board members
and their associates was partly rooted in their desire to
influence the disposition of jobs.

If the Anglo-Saxons who dominated local politics at the
start of the nineteenth century were able to move aside for
the Irish in New York, Boston, and other large cities, leaving
in their place large numbers of Irish civil servants, the ethnic
strategy of the 1960s faced more formidable obstacles.
Whether the Irish still dominated or newer ethnic groups had
moved into control as did the Italians and the Jews in New
York City, the black and Spanish-speaking population in the
1960s found seizing political control and assuming control
of the bureaucracies impossible to achieve.

Still, as the community action programs began to falter
toward the end of the 1960s, the black and Spanish-speaking
groups were not willing to give up the public service jobs
they had achieved nor the political power they had begun to
exercise. Many of these demands and frustrations became
merged in the concept of community control.

Demands for community control were particularly
emphatic within the large city school systems of the country.
In Detroit, Los Angeles, Washington, D.C., St. Louis, and
New York, where black and Hispanic groups represented a
sizable proportion of the school and general population,
these demands took on particular force. In its original form,
community control meant the creation of individual schools
and groups of schools that would be run by local citizens,
independently of the larger school system. Many of the
individuals who had been active in community corporations

turned toward education as an urban bureaucracy particularly receptive to their influence. A ready constituency existed among the parents of schoolchildren of the new ethnic groups. As the concentration of black and Spanish-speaking children in these large city school systems increased, the logic of community control became more compelling.

The most publicized early ventures in community control were the three demonstration districts created in New York City with the aid of the Ford Foundation. These districts, Ocean Hill–Brownsville (in Brooklyn) and IS 201 and Two Bridges (in Harlem and on the Lower East Side in Manhattan), consisted of junior high schools and elementary feeder schools. Along with community schools in St. Louis and Washington, they formed the beginning of a movement which led to demands for full-scale decentralization. State legislatures in Michigan, New York, and California considered formal decentralization legislation, with plans for Detroit and New York City having actually been enacted.

In examining this phenomenon of community control with particular reference to Ocean Hill–Brownsville, its sources, manifestations, and developments will be considered. Community control was at once a tactic of ethnic assertion and a focal point for the increasing ethnicity that affected educational politics during the 1960s. Yet to understand the movement fully, it must be placed within the context of school systems pervaded by ethnic considerations. When the school systems in New York and Detroit were legislatively decentralized and when the school system in Los Angeles was left unchanged, state legislatures were responding to the dilemmas of community control in their own measured ways. Dencentralization was both an offering to the proponents of ethnic assertiveness and an attempt to mute the ethnic conflict which community control symbolized.

The ethnic conflict in New York City was perhaps the most

dramatic. It was also openly acknowledged by the local
political leaders as their reason for adopting legislation to
decentralize the school system. This ready acceptance of
the ethnic dimensions of decentralization are reflected in the
membership of the Interim Board of Education for the City
of New York (1969), a group created to oversee the shift to
decentralization. Each of the five members of the Interim
Board was appointed by a borough president. Herman
Badillo, the Puerto Rican borough president of the Bronx,
appointed a Puerto Rican, Joseph Monserrat. Robert Connor,
the Irish Catholic borough president of Staten Island,
appointed an Irish Catholic, Mary E. Meade. Sidney Leviss,
the Jewish borough president of Queens, appointed Murry
Bergtraum, a Jew. Abe Stark, the Jewish borough president
of Brooklyn, appointed Seymour Lachman, a Jew. And Percy
Sutton, the black borough president of Manhattan, appointed
Isaiah Robinson, a black.

While the particular configuration of ethnic representation
was somewhat a question of circumstance, the importance
of ethnic balancing is beyond question. In 1947, when the
membership of the New York City Board of Education was
increased from seven to nine, it was generally understood
as an accommodation to provide equal representation of
Catholics, Jews, and Protestants. This kind of ethnic
representation was certainly on the minds of those who
drafted the decentralization legislation in 1969.

Community control, then, was but the most salient
indicator in the 1960s and 1970s that ethnicity still shaped
educational policy. In fact, in most major policy areas, big
city education was affected by the competing demands of
ethnic groups. Educational reform, for example, not only
involved demands for ethnically oriented curricula, but often
became an alternative to ethnic confrontation. If the school
community could be mobilized in behalf of educational
reform, that community might be less divided by ethnic

conflict. Student rights, which at times rivaled community control for media attention, involved a fascinating interplay between the white and black student activists who sought to develop a common agenda. Was free speech, crucial to the mostly white student newspaper editors, more important than due process in suspensions, always a serious issue with black student activists? To what extent should the protections of free speech be limited by avoidance of racially and religiously inflammatory statements? Even an issue as seemingly innocuous as streamlining the bureaucracy was thoroughly immersed in ethnic considerations. Changes in the bureaucratic structure inevitably affected senior personnel who often represented ethnic constituencies.

Ironically, if the demands of the black and Hispanic groups for community control dominated the 1960s, the 1970s were highlighted by the demands of white ethnic groups for community control, often to resist integration, busing, and adverse zoning. The responses of groups in the South Boston sections of Boston, the Canarsie section of Brooklyn, and throughout the country once again brought the ethnic issue to the forefront of education policy. Ethnic organization, for good or bad, is a fact of life in many of the largest cities in this country. In big city politics its impact is perhaps most pronounced on the educational bureaucracy. And ethnic organization is not likely to disappear. Indeed, the evidence indicates that it is spreading to affect education in the middle-size cities and suburban areas traditionally thought to be immune from ethnic conflict.

The American educational system is the most far-reaching and pervasive manifestation of governmental power in this country. It is fiscally the greatest concern of state and local governments, with over one-third of their allocations going to education. It has enjoyed a rich, perhaps unique, history of citizen control and involvement, one which is marveled at throughout the world. Yet the costs of citizen involvement have often been division and conflict.

Even so, experiences during the 1960s and 1970s have shown that the competition among ethnic groups within the educational system need not always be ruinous. Educators and government officials are constantly challenged to deal with ethnicity in creative ways. We offer here no easy prescriptions. But a careful review of the community control controversy, as well as several other major educational controversies of this period, will serve as a basis for coming to grips with the dimensions of ethnicity in education. In each instance, an overview of the particular controversy will be highlighted by an in-depth study focusing on the New York City experience and drawing upon our firsthand knowledge and confidential records. In this way the abstractions of ethnic politics will take on the reality of day-to-day school operations and transmit the excitement and drama that ethnic groups bring to education.

For a time, during the 1960s, it looked as if ethnic conflict might damage public education seriously. Perhaps, instead, these lessons of the past decades will lead to a new appreciation of the depth and richness that America's diverse ethnic heritage can bring to public education and, indeed, to all its institutions.

The End of Ocean Hill–Brownsville

Along Rockaway, Atlantic, and Hopkinson avenues in Brooklyn, the neighborhood had been for as long as one could remember Italian-American. The vegetable stores, the barber shops—where on Saturday afternoons one could still hear the radio broadcast of the operas, the smell of strong red wines, sausages, and cheeses—all were nearly gone by the middle of the 1960s. The newcomers who slipped into the old, often decrepit four-story walk-ups were, as in many similar areas in the big cities, overwhelmingly black and Puerto Rican. Ocean Hill was no exception.

It was equally true of Brownsville. Separated from Ocean Hill by Eastern Parkway and reaching for many street blocks into a formerly Jewish community, it had become one of the most ravaged sections in the nation: garbage everywhere, abandoned houses, terrorized populations, with the very few remaining stores shielded by iron gates. Police prowl cars patrolled street after street leveled by housing authorities and wandering wreckers, past rubble-strewn lots interspersed with dilapidated buildings. No one could view this area and not think of the bombed cities of Coventry, Dresden, and Hiroshima.

Given these disasters, many people began a search for the sources of their discontent. But who was the enemy? The police? Sanitation workers? The White House? And even if they were, what precisely would help Ocean Hill–Brownsville?

By 1968, an old red brick home for wayward Catholic girls (with shattered glass atop its ten-foot brick walls) was gone, and in its place stood Atlantic Plaza Towers, a middle-income cooperative housing complex. On its main floor were the offices of the Ocean Hill–Brownsville Unit Administrator, Rhody McCoy, and his governing board.

A story was told by old-timers around the Board of Education's central headquarters about the district's conception. One day Superintendent of Schools Bernard Donovan decided to yield to the pressures to establish "demonstration" school districts. Donovan named one of his close associates to carry out his plan. Another longtime school administrator asked Donovan's appointee, almost a year before the crippling autumn 1968 teachers' strike, whether there were any ground rules for the operations. "Any notion of what it can and cannot do?" he asked. Donovan's aide and friend had first entered the school system nearly thirty years earlier on the crest of the Irish take-over of the schools from the Protestants.

"Plans? Guidelines? What the hell are you talking about? Who needs any?"

He had total faith in Donovan's resiliency, his seemingly congenital ability to weave and bob and improvise, telling competing groups what they wanted to hear and, despite regular contradictions, never getting caught. Like Talleyrand, people mused, often in awe, Bernie Donovan lived on. And he nearly did—except that, in the end, the strike almost brought the entire system and the city down.

In Ocean Hill–Brownsville, most people defined their demonstration district in whatever way they wished. Surely, those who reached for power there reasoned, life would be better with it. But power, of course, did corrupt and the responsibilities of that power were frequently overwhelming. Once in office, they would have to deliver and, failing that, they would have to cope with their own opposition, equally poor and nonwhite, and just as bitter.

When the members of the Interim Board of Education arrived in 1969—a board created by the new state decentralization law—the issue was whether the demonstration districts ought to live or die. The teachers' strike had led to the formation of the Interim Board as a "temporary" measure. The state legislature, in an indirect slap at Mayor John V. Lindsay, gave the five borough presidents the power to name the new Board. And, unlike Board members on previous school boards, the newcomers had the ability to make some things happen, if only because the new law gave them more authority than their predecessors.

In Brooklyn, the venerable Abe Stark presided over Borough Hall. He was best known for his famous sign at the base of Ebbets Field's right field: HIT SIGN, WIN A SUIT. (No one ever had.) Stark once owned a men's clothing store, ironically a few moments' walk from the Ocean Hill–Brownsville district office. His Board appointee, Seymour Lachman, was a college dean and a history professor. His background and experience as an educator in intergroup relations and his awareness of the competition among ethnic groups led him to stress reconciliation and the development of moderate leadership.

Murry Bergtraum, the Queens appointee, had spent many years in school affairs. He was a leader among the local school board advisory members who had fought for greater powers and independent legislative authority.

Joseph Monserrat represented the Bronx. He was Puerto Rican–born, handsome, with grayish white curly hair, a former social worker who had once run the Commonwealth of Puerto Rico's Office of Migration, the virtual embassy of desperately impoverished emigrants to the world outside the *barrio.*

The fourth member was Isaiah Robinson, more conservative than many of his fellow blacks who urged him on. One had only to observe him during the Board's private sessions to recognize that he was no believer in revolutionary change. Robinson never questioned the basic tenets of the system; he merely wanted in for himself and his people. Genuinely committed, an intensely moral man, he often seemed almost apolitical. His efforts on the Board seemed hampered by this hesitancy to engage in the day-to-day politics that success would often require.

The Staten Island representative was Mary E. Meade, Irish-Catholic, a schoolteacher for almost half a century, appointed, in 1937, the first woman principal of a New York City coeducational high school, and, until her retirement in 1965, administrative head of the city's centralized high schools in Manhattan and Staten Island.

James Regan would come to the Board as Meade's successor in July 1972, when she was dropped by the borough president.

Young, ambitious, personable, he was a onetime high school teacher who had earlier run for Democratic party county leader on Staten Island and lost. Politics was his life, his calendar crowded with breakfasts, luncheons, and dinners (almost all on "his" island), his itinerary outside the

city filled with conferences and meetings with political
contacts. His office at 110 Livingston Street might become a
springboard to other things.

A few days after the new Board was inducted, McCoy
called Lachman. Could he visit with them at the district
offices?

This was Lachman's first meeting with Rhody McCoy, a
placid-looking, middle-aged veteran of the system who
quietly puffed on his pipe between introductions to the
members of the governing board and its chairman, the
Reverend C. Herbert Oliver. A half-hour before, Oliver, a
handsome, Southern Baptist minister once active in Martin
Luther King's civil rights movement, had been strolling in the
halls of a local school when a boy ran up to him.

"Reverend Oliver, Reverend Oliver," he said, "please give
me your autograph. Please?"

The dignified, always immaculate Oliver removed his pen
carefully from his breast pocket and signed.

"Wow," the boy shrieked as he started to leave. "Wow, my
grandmother'll never believe this."

The talk that first day began slowly, each of them feeling
the others out. Obviously, McCoy's and Oliver's concern was
the preservation of the demonstration project. "What are you
going to do for us?" they demanded to know, not unkindly.
"Sentence us to death? You're clearly one of *them* or else
you wouldn't have been appointed." Lachman, ignoring the
questions, said little. "Let's take a walking tour of your
schools," he said. "Let's begin to see what you've
accomplished." He was particularly interested in visiting
JHS 271, about which many of the worst storms of the past
year had swirled, with repeated charges that two black
teachers, Leslie Campbell and Albert Vann, had created a
mad-hatter's world there.

Not until two hours later, after the students and most of

the teachers had left for the day, was Lachman brought to the school. There was little to see. Bulletin boards. Notices. Empty, still halls and classrooms. He came away uneasy: Was there anything to hide? Was something going on? What, then?

At the end of the tour, Oliver turned directly to Lachman. More than McCoy, perhaps more than any other member of the governing board, C. Herbert Oliver was a man of presence, developed during his earlier ministry in Birmingham, Alabama. Sadly, almost diffidently, and with a habitual softness in his voice, he asked, "What will you do with our demonstration district?"

Oliver pressed him. Would Lachman "tear it apart and throw it to the winds?"

"No," he answered. "No, not at all. That would be unwise and unfortunate. I personally favor one large and expanded Ocean Hill–Brownsville District with at least 20,000 average daily population, as the new decentralization law requires."

Oliver said nothing. At no time during that first day had he suggested the demonstration district with its 7,000 students be preserved as an isolated ward of the system. All he wanted was that the district be kept alive, in once piece—if necessary, within a larger contiguous area.

It was also during those early first weeks that Lachman met Sam Wright, Democratic party leader of the district and state assemblyman. An early proponent of the demonstration district, he had quickly veered from it, bitterly opposing the people on its governing board and the direction they had taken.

Everybody had an opinion about Sam Wright. A Democratic party politician said,

Sam has a penchant for maneuvering like a great broken-field runner. You never know when he'll break for a long one on you. You think you've got him and then,

whammo, he springs a wild multi-million dollar project on
the Mayor and the press and public and even gets a *Times*
editorial praising him for his vision. You think that no one
will talk to him in the black community and then one day
you discover that he is admired for making it. He's taken
on everyone in Brownsville and still he regularly comes
out on top. Everyone says he's hated, yet he wins elections
easily. He would become president of his community
school board, maybe the city's most retarded district in
the 3 R's. Bad, huh? But who does he bring to a meeting
of the 100 Black Men? None other than Schools Chancellor
Harvey Scribner, who made his living identifying himself
with Wright's enemies.

There was this, too, about Wright: He was at times
shrewder than his rivals. Soon after his first visit, his wife
appeared at central headquarters (in her capacity as
president of JHS 271's PTA) with seven other parents of
children in the district's schools. Did the Board realize what
was going on in the very school their own flesh and blood
attended? There was terror, screamed one woman, "They
have been teaching those kids to hate." She produced a
written document, protesting the governing board:

1. We, the parents of the children of the schools don't
    have a voice in the community of school affairs.
2. We were not consulted on the commencement plans.
3. We and our children were harassed, beaten and
    threatened. We have reported several incidents to the
    police department and yet nothing was done.
4. The kids are turned on by Leslie Campbell against the
    UFT teachers and then Campbell can't control them,
    with the kids frequently running amok.

And they recommended—

1. that [the] JHS 271 principal be dismissed.
2. that every effort be made to bring in "licensed and qualified teachers."
3. that [Leslie] Campbell and [Albert] Vann, who are "ripping the school apart," be dismissed.

Not long afterward, Lachman again visited the Ocean Hill schools. Oliver passed by and Lachman moved toward him. Why was he permitting a professional to control his governing board? Lachman asked. McCoy seems to be the dominant figure in your schools. How would it appear if the superintendent of schools controlled the central Board? This, said Lachman openly, was his impression of their power relationship.

Oliver waved him away. "That's not true," he insisted; "that's not true at all. The governing board made the decisions and McCoy only carried them out."

It was 1:30 in the afternoon and Hopkinson Avenue was quiet, with only a few cars passing by. New trees had been planted at Atlantic Towers. The tenants took a fierce pride in the limited comforts that a life of hard work had brought to them and their young. So did McCoy, who had spent nearly twenty years in the system and had become convinced that poor black children were deliberately being slighted. They were certainly not being taught as well as middle-income youngsters, but the larger question had less to do with culprits and scapegoats than with another kind of reality: Given the existing state of knowledge of the learning process and the interrelationship among whites *and* nonwhites, how did one reverse the trend toward continued retardation? If Ocean Hill–Brownsville and the other demonstration districts had any rationale for remaining alive, it was in making discernible progress with their students' mastery of basic skills. The political in-fighting was debilitating, but the

System, nameless and faceless and ever-so-elastic, could
live through attack and counterattack. The children of Ocean
Hill–Brownsville could not.

McCoy and Lachman were two minor actors in a
monumental tragedy. One lived with the pain of American
slavery, the other with the awareness of what it meant to be
a Jew in a Christian world. They should have been allies but
events had drawn them apart. At the very best, they and their
sympathizers would have to learn soon to coexist.

The controversy over Ocean Hill–Brownsville and the
demonstration districts had its origins in the escalating
demands for the decentralization of the largest school
system in the country. Toward the latter part of the 1950s,
the movement toward local control received a strong boost,
when the existing Board of Education was charged with
inefficiency, wrongdoing, and corruption. The Board was
empowered to appoint local school boards that would
assume advisory powers designed "to allow the maximum
possible participation by the people of the city of New York
in the affairs of the city school system."

In an effort to create a new type of local school board, this
Board of Education adopted, on April 4, 1962, a "Plan for the
Revitalization of Local School Boards," which called for the
establishment of nine-member local boards in each field
superintendent's area, of which there were 25. These local
boards became an important force in the mushrooming
movement toward decentralization of the school system.

In the fall of 1965, the Board of Education approved an
increase in the number of districts from 25 to 30 and
increased the powers of the superintendents in charge of the
districts. The decrease in the size of the largest districts was
an important step toward creating a more uniform district
system that would lend itself to greater local autonomy.
Although, in the spring of 1966, one civic group lamented

that progress toward the Board's announced goal of decentralization "has certainly been slow," the pace thereafter began to accelerate.

During its next phase, decentralization became enmeshed in increasing political conflict, controversy over the state aid formula, and a strengthened movement for popular participation, benefiting from the new concern for community power.

During the spring of 1966, newly elected Mayor John V. Lindsay began defining his own relationship to the school system in a way that differed markedly from the hands-off approach of his predecessor, Mayor Robert F. Wagner.

Up until the spring of 1967, the mayor merely prodded the Board of Education to greater efforts at reorganization. During the 1967 legislative session, however, in agreeing to a revised state aid formula that would provide greater funds for New York City, the legislative leaders required the mayor to submit to its next session a plan for meaningful decentralization of the New York City school system. This task might have remained a perfunctory exercise, but for several fortuitous developments. Members of the existing local school boards were becoming impatient with their lack of power. Partisans of the newly created demonstration districts began pressing for greater "community control" over education. Continuing conflict between the mayor and the Board of Education began to serve as a catalytic agent to change processes within the educational system.

The requirement that the mayor prepare a report to the legislature was perceived by Mayor Lindsay as an opportunity to gain greater control over the school system. It also enabled him to satisfy the demand of certain elements of the black and Puerto Rican populations for greater community control. Mayor Lindsay appointed McGeorge Bundy, the new president of the Ford Foundation, to head a

commission to make recommendations for the reorganization
of the New York City school system. Concomitantly, the Ford
Foundation provided funds for the planning of three
experimental districts in Ocean Hill–Brownsville, Harlem
(IS 201), and lower Manhattan (Two Bridges). During the
summer and fall of 1967, while the Bundy commission was
developing its proposals, the experimental districts began
operating and were soon involved in negotiations with the
Board of Education about their exact status and power. The
demonstration districts came to symbolize the demand of
the black and Puerto Rican inner-city populations for a
greater share in governmental decision making. They raised
the issue of increased local control to the point where it
could no longer be ignored.

With the publication of the Bundy report in November
1967, the demand for radical reorganization of the school
system received considerable impetus. Mayor Lindsay's
advocacy of major reorganization brought the issue to the
1968 session of the New York State legislature. What began,
during the 1968 session, as a conflict between the mayor and
the Board of Education, involving two approaches to the
reorganization of the city school system, became, during the
1969 session, a struggle between two coalitions, involving a
large number of private groups and governmental units. By
the beginning of the 1969 session, the coalitions reflected
the growing cleavages among the political and social forces
throughout New York City. A great many leaders became
emotionally and personally involved in the advocacy of their
positions. By the time legislation was passed, many
friendships had been severely strained. The 1969 legislation,
although it failed to resolve many of the substantive issues,
returned the reorganization controversy to New York City
and a new five-member Interim Board of Education.

The most immediate and direct impact of the school
reorganization law was the creation of a new institutional

framework for education in New York City. An Interim Board
of Education was established, with representatives
appointed by the borough presidents of the five boroughs
of New York City. In their initial appointments, each borough
president had reflected his own ethnic and religious ties. In
practice the main responsibility of the Interim Board during
its first six months became the preparation of a tentative
districting plan to define the boundaries of each community
district, which would elect its own community board with
authority over the schools below the high school level.
Perhaps the most difficult and the most controversial
problem before the Interim Board was the status of the
demonstration districts. As with many controversial matters,
this one was avoided. The 1969 legislation simply omitted
any reference to the demonstration districts.

By the end of 1969 and into 1970, the issue was whether
the three demonstration districts ought to be preserved.
Moving away from demonstrations and sit-ins, supporters of
the districts began to argue that the state legislature's
decentralization law allowed them to continue, even though
a school district required a minimum of 20,000 students.
This was also Isaiah Robinson's view.

People were called in to advise the members. The Board's
special counsel on decentralization was queried, and his
consistent reply was that the legislature meant no such thing.
Lachman's special assistant Murray Polner spoke with
people generally favorable to the district, most notably with
Ira Glasser, director of the New York Civil Liberties Union.
"Even so staunch a friend of the demonstration districts as
the NYCLU now believes it is not possible to preserve them
legally," he reported.

The pressures were building. What would the Board do
when it proposed its redistricting plan? Would it keep the
demonstration districts? Merge them into larger districts?
Or dismember them entirely?

The *New York Times* ran a lengthy piece on the subject.
"Ocean Hill at Peace: Involved and Frustrated," its headline
read. The story claimed there was a determined "community
effort" to keep it alive. McCoy had launched a national
publicity campaign. Educators as far removed from the
scene as Massachusetts and Arkansas uncritically praised
his innovations as major advances in urban education.
Translated, that was supposed to mean to the unsophisticated
that McCoy was unraveling the secret: how to school the
dispossessed in our Northern city and Southern rural
schools. It was reason enough for many black parents to
come to the defense of Ocean Hill. At least something was
being tried. Lachman was as confused as anyone else. He
invited the Brooklyn delegation of the state legislature to
meet with him. Virtually all the legislators insisted that the
intent in Albany had been clear. Each district had to have
20,000 average daily attendance in its schools. No fewer.

Still, Lachman tried. He talked with assembly minority
leader Stanley Steingut. He met with the black caucus. Sam
Wright exploded. The preservation of the demonstration
districts would mean segregation, and Wright said he wanted
integrated schools. "They're preaching hate," he said with
fury, slamming his fist against the table. "Hate against white
people and against America. It is destroying the city."

"But Sam," someone interrupted, "why not whip them
once and for all during the election? You run for the school
board. You'll beat them easily. You've been saying that for
two years now, that you could win any election held in Ocean
Hill."

Wright was annoyed. "Ah, come on, now," he said, in his
discernible Brooklyn accent. "That was true then, but now
I'm not so sure. Rhody receives $4 million of State Urban
Education funds for his Community Education Centers.
These people are now on his payroll—hundreds of them—
they're dependent on him for jobs. You know what that

means? How can I, a district leader and assemblyman, compete with his power structure?"

McCoy felt the same way. Shortly before he had been asked why, if he had such popular support in the community, he didn't run for the local school board against Wright? McCoy laughed. "Who could beat Sam Wright's machine?"

The black politicians were no help. Off the record they agreed with Wright and saw Ocean Hill as a threat to their careers. Publicly, they held their tongues.

The pressure mounted.

Shirley Chisholm privately damned Ocean Hill's leadership: The children weren't learning, she said. But she also warned of "blood in the streets."

Stanley Steingut wanted the demonstration districts killed. But his mind dwelt less on their fate than on a group of Democratic insurgents preparing to oppose him in the primary and the fact that East Flatbush and Crown Heights, his areas, were rapidly losing their white majority. Who knows? A black area might someday demand a black representative in Albany.

At a Catholic Teachers Association luncheon one Sunday, teachers union leader Albert Shanker made it clear he would accept nothing less than the death of Ocean Hill–Brownsville. There was no room for compromise. Lachman recalled that he phoned Bergtraum a few evenings later and told him that he was beginning to waver. One of the mayor's Urban Task Force leaders had privately urged him to destroy Ocean Hill–Brownsville, to "prevent its pus from spilling over into the rest of the city." Now Lachman was telling Bergtraum, who was readying the majority statement incorporating the districts into larger ones, of his growing doubts, of his anxieties about racial conflict. Bergtraum hung up, upset. He had three votes. If Lachman took a walk, then McCoy would win.

Lachman called Monserrat to say he was reconsidering

his vote. If he did not, it would appear that the vote was
along racial lines—three whites versus one black and one
Puerto Rican. Moreover, the case for either decision was not
that overwhelmingly cogent. The next day Monserrat called.
Shanker and Senator Earl Brydges, Republican majority
leader of the New York State Senate, had given him a
warning: If you dare to keep the districts alive, Albany will
turn its back on the city. And no more extra time to make
your decision, either, they warned. In fact, they might even
have to attack the members publicly. Monserrat, shaken,
now began to reconsider his own position.

Shortly thereafter, Lachman had an unexpected visitor,
Sam Wright's associate and law partner. He was carrying a
personal letter from Wright. It was in Wright's handwriting.

Please forgive my intrusion. . . . However, the emergency
of this matter and the meeting of the Board with the Mayor
dictates this note. . . . Congresswoman Chisholm . . . would
like to discuss with you the situation before your meeting
with the Mayor. . . . She is expecting your call and has
indicated being in favor of the option of allowing the
locally elected board to decide on the continuation of the
experimental district. We are all in favor of doing what is
best for the children. Here certainly is the opportunity to
have the parents and other community residents decide
what is best for the children.

The letter betrayed Wright's desperation. Lachman then
contacted Shirley Chisholm directly. They had known one
another for several years, ever since she had been in Albany
as an assemblywoman. Chisholm said the critical question
for her was whether the local community would decide the
future of Ocean Hill–Brownsville. While she favored the
larger Brownsville district, she could not call for it openly,

because that might be interpreted as being against community control.

Lachman drove to Gracie Mansion, where the Board met with Mayor Lindsay. Lindsay was worried, concerned, and exhausted. He had just come through a bruising reelection campaign. In response to a query from Monserrat, Lindsay said it was his position that the demonstration districts had been ruled out by the last session of the legislature. "Nothing can be done to change this," he said, "regardless of our personal opinion." According to Lindsay, the legislation was precise in its intent. As the meeting broke up, Lachman mentioned privately to Lindsay that a mutual friend, a respected judge, had recently rendered a different opinion informally. The mayor replied, "I respect him a great deal but he is wrong on this issue. We have no room for movement." He then went on to repeat that the legislative intent was to destroy the demonstration districts, and "we have no alternative but to follow the law." He concluded, "We cannot continue them. We fought against it, but they decided to do this anyway. Furthermore," Lindsay said, "Shanker has warned that if the demonstration districts are continued there will be utter chaos. He said he felt there would be more disruption if we retained them than if we gave them up."

The following morning, Lachman received another call from Sam Wright. He said that, on Monday morning, fifty people would be sitting-in at his office and they would then go to Monserrat's office and do the same. Wright said that the sitters-ins were hard-working people who lived in the Ocean Hill community but did not have jobs on Rhody McCoy's payroll. He claimed that they were upset and were going to explode. Soon, he predicted, they would turn to violence, a claim made repeatedly and mindlessly by many people on both sides of the issue throughout those years.

That same day Lachman drove into the city for a meeting

with the New York Board of Rabbis. This had been arranged
when his position was beginning to loosen, and he wanted
the rabbis to know that some of the issues involving the
demonstration districts were ambiguous. He wanted to
persuade them to respect his judgment, regardless of his
decision.

Two of the rabbis present took the position that perhaps
the maintenance of the demonstration districts in their
present form or in some other form might be better than
getting rid of them, because their dismemberment could
bring more tension and greater confrontation to the city. But
others disagreed.

Oddly enough, the most strenuous disagreement came
from two Reform rabbis. Lachman was quite surprised
because both had been involved with the first school
integration attempts in New York City. One who had been
involved in the writing of the Ford Foundation's (Bundy)
report on decentralization seemed to have changed his
attitude because of the failure of integration and the growth
of black separatism.

Meanwhile, another rabbi speculated that because the
Brooklyn Diocese of the Catholic Church wasn't directly
involved, the church didn't care what the decision of the
Board would be. But the Protestant churches of Brooklyn, he
argued, was committed to the preservation of Ocean Hill.
The Italian-American community was more concerned with
busing and the arrival of black students in their areas
through open enrollment. Whites in the borough, he
reasoned, would not care too much if the demonstration
districts were preserved so long as there was peace in the
city and so long as their schools were not harmed.

Several of the rabbis offered to use their excellent political
contacts to pressure city and state officials to issue public
statements against the demonstration districts.

Lachman was more determined than ever to prevent the

Board of Education from polarizing along racial lines on this issue. The three white members of the Board must not be opposed to the black and Puerto Rican members of the Board on an issue that had divided the city in similar fashion just a year earlier.

A few days later Wright's sitters-in stormed the eleventh floor. They accused McCoy of running a "black mafia," of using "Gestapo tactics," of mismanaging funds, and of spreading racial hatred among their children. It was that kind of civil war.

Not long afterward, Lachman again visited IS 271. As he walked into the principal's office, there sat, on either side of the long, rectangular table, the antagonists, all shrieking at one another. Charges and countercharges, of graft, narcotics peddling, and addiction, of unruly students, of impotent parent associations, and of pervasive and endemic violence within the school, surfaced once more. The principal tried to pacify first one side and then the other. His aim, however, was quite distant from that of the debaters. Sometime earlier he had told Lachman that while Campbell and Vann were a major problem, he personally didn't care whether 271 was in the demonstration district or in a larger Brownsville school district. What really mattered to him, as mattered to many professionals, was what would happen to the demonstration school principals who had risked their careers when they joined forces with Rhody McCoy?

Demonstration followed counterdemonstration, and there were repeated incursions into central headquarters. Robinson became incensed. "I can't get any work done," he said in one of his rare flashes of anger. Soon after that, the Board initiated a strict security system. Thereafter, no one was permitted on the tenth and eleventh floors—where the chancellor and the Board were quartered—without a specific invitation. One elevator was reserved for those floors, and all doors were sealed.

Monserrat called Lachman. He had, he said, just met with
Ocean Hill's governing board and was again doubtful. "I
dunno. They keep telling me how wonderful they're doing
with the kids." He worried that none of the new educational
practices they raved about had yet been judged in any way.
"I know, Joe, I know," Lachman told him. "A week ago I
might have bought that line and gone along with you. But
we have discussed this time and again and have already
come to an informal four-to-one decision. Everything's at the
printers. We've only got forty hours before the press
conference. If you start now with this change of heart, it
could disrupt the city again. And, anyway, remember how
McCoy wouldn't let us evaluate his programs? Rhody is
afraid we'll find out that he hasn't done anything anyone else
hasn't done."

Lachman couldn't sleep well that night, brooding over
indecision and his own fallibility. His small son was ill with
a cold, and Lachman kept walking into his son's bedroom,
thinking more of his own problems than of the boy. At seven
in the morning, he could barely contain himself. No one
answered Monserrat's phone at that hour. But an hour later
he tried again.

Monserrat sounded tired, even remote, and almost timid.
The way someone must sound after taking an awful
pounding. Monserrat said he was going to go along with the
majority decision. The demonstration districts would be
absorbed into larger districts, which would then decide for
themselves whether or not they wanted to keep them going.

It seemed all over then, but McCoy and Oliver and their
supporters refused to concede. What was going to happen
within the next six weeks was an understandable, if
mismanaged, publicity campaign to get the members to
change their minds. Two votes were all they needed. "Just
you watch," said Marjorie Matthews, a wise and experienced
black member of the neighboring Bedford-Stuyvesant school

board, "we will now witness a struggle for power that hasn't a thing to do with children—only a desire to hold on to economic and political power."

Lachman had sent an observer into Ocean Hill as well as into other poor ghetto districts, and he believed that McCoy had nothing going on in his classrooms different from other nonwhite classrooms. Many of his well-publicized innovations had already taken root in other less favored, less romanticized nonwhite schools. And, finally, Lachman reached yet another conclusion, one that would dispel whatever remaining doubts he had.

Several weeks earlier, he had had an idea: Why not ask Louis Harris, the pollster, to conduct a survey in Ocean Hill–Brownsville? Lachman had met Harris several weeks earlier at a Ford Foundation conference. The study would be secret, with no leaks to the press. It was to be funded by the foundation, and Vice-President Mitchell Sviridoff suggested that Kenneth B. Clark's Metropolitan Applied Research Center act as a conduit. Clark agreed.

In a draft letter, dated November 24, 1969, Lachman wrote:

I would like a survey conducted in the area served by the eight schools of the Ocean Hill–Brownsville demonstration district to determine whether the people want (1) to remain as a demonstration district under the authority of the Central Board and the Chancellor; (2) to continue as a demonstration district, but be included in an enlarged Brownsville school district, under the authority of a newly elected community school board; (3) to become part of a larger Brownsville district without any differentiation between the Ocean Hill schools and the other Brownsville schools in the new district.

I would also like the survey to test whether or not parents of children currently in the eight schools believe their children's education to have been improved, retarded, or the same as before, and the reasons they gave. I think the study should give us some idea of how parents and community residents perceive well-known personalities associated with this project or the area which services the demonstration district, e.g., Rhody McCoy, the Reverend Oliver, Shirley Chisholm, Leslie Campbell, Albert Vann, John Lindsay, Sam Wright, and others, and how they really feel about the experiment.

If the results showed that the experiment was clearly and widely supported by its constituency—as its proponents claimed was the case—and if the public hearings on the districts substantiated those findings, then, Lachman said, he would change his mind and vote to allow it to survive as an independent entity.

Only black and Puerto Rican interviewers were used. Besides himself and Polner, only Harris; one of his vice-presidents, Mike Edison; and Professor Bert Swanson, a sociologist at Sarah Lawrence College, would be closely involved in the study. Swanson was recommended by Harris. He had been used for a similar poll taken in Ocean Hill–Brownsville before the strike, in the spring of 1968, as well as for a second poll during the strike, in December 1968.

The results of the study were never released publicly, but what it determined was that the overwhelming majority interviewed did not care whether Ocean Hill lived or died or was absorbed. Thirty-five percent of those interviewed thought their children were receiving excellent to pretty good educations; 61 percent (up 3 percent from December 1968) believed otherwise. Sixty-eight percent said the schools were the same or worse.

Principals and teachers were more willing to talk with parents now, but a staggering number of respondents believed there had been no improvement in student discipline or reported that the failure to improve reading scores remained a source of great uneasiness to them. Forty-two percent viewed the governing board favorably and 32 percent did not. McCoy and Chisholm were tied in popularity at 54 percent, Oliver had 38 percent, and Wright received only 14 percent.

The passions of the strike had naturally created greater support for the experiment, but in time that, too, passed—so much so that 60 percent of the population (and 66 percent of the blacks) said they would gladly sacrifice the experiment for better schooling for their young. The verdict was that despite his personal popularity, Rhody McCoy's Ocean Hill–Brownsville experimental district had no clear-cut support. Of those polled, 36 percent said they were "hesitant" about openly criticizing Ocean Hill for fear of reprisals.

When rumors spread that the experiment would be enlarged to include some schools from Bedford-Stuyvesant's adjoining and equally nonwhite district, there was an angry protest from Bedford-Stuyvesant parent representatives of an all-black school board, dubious about both McCoy's grandiose claims and his white supporters' "proofs" of his success. They wanted, they said, "real education and the opportunity for our children to learn." Nothing more nor less. It was class and race and hopes and history and fears. The more privileged white simplifiers saw it as reverse racism; those who had all their lives lived with the pain of rejection and the apprehension of defeat saw it as less an exercise in guilt feeling and ideology than as a personal necessity. The children, after all, were their own.

In the end, one demonstration district, IS 201 in Harlem, was allowed to live on by the newly created and enlarged Harlem district (but only for one more year). Another, Two

Bridges in lower Manhattan, was condemned by nearly all and died unmourned. Ocean Hill–Brownsville also died, rejected by the larger school district in which its schools lay.

The struggle for the demonstration districts represented the confluence in New York City of black and Hispanic demands for community control with the theoretical justification of academics like Richard Cloward and Marilyn Gittell and the funding support of the Ford Foundation. New York City's demonstration districts became the focal point for a national awakening on the part of the black and Hispanic minorities throughout the country.

Community control as a strategy for transferring power to the new ethnic groups was successful in some ways. It certainly mobilized the new ethnic communities, often through conflict with existing groups. It also, however, produced a countermobilization among those ethnic groups dominant in urban and school politics. Canarsie, the subject of a later chapter, can be viewed as a reaction to Ocean Hill–Brownsville.

Certainly, community control and decentralization efforts, in part, moved from the city to the state legislature in New York, Michigan, and California because the older ethnic groups in these states sought to bolster their own positions. New ethnic groups using decentralization as a political strategy face the danger of countermobilization and the escalation of conflict to arenas such as state legislatures where the previously dominant groups are more powerful.

Nonetheless, the creation of the demonstration districts and then of the community school districts in New York City and the creation of smaller school districts in Detroit and Washington and other cities has accelerated the pace at which new ethnics became teachers and administrators.

Decentralization's greatest failures may reside in the bloated expectations that accompany its advocacy and the disappointment of those who think that decentralization

will alter the basic character of American education. But
the central bureaucracy, though attenuated, still exists even
with decentralization. Additional district bureaucracies were
created. School personnel still remained largely the same,
and classroom and school building organization was not
altered. Militant exponents of community control argue to
this day that their efforts never really received a fair trial,
since neighborhood people were never sufficiently involved.
But even if radical decentralization to individual school units
run by neighborhood boards had been adopted, would these
changes have affected the character of the school system?
And what would have been the effect of those changes on the
quality of education? Aren't the critics of decentralization
closer to the truth when they argue that a national system
of education is really at work, using textbooks produced by
national publishers and increasingly dominated by the mass
media, while also subject to state and federal bodies and
national unions, all of which make dreams of radical
decentralization hopelessly romantic.

3

Beating the Bureaucracy

Benefiting from the image of large-scale organization in need of therapeutic fracturing, community control and decentralization of schools became the watchwords of the late 1960s. Almost every major city in the country, including Detroit, Los Angeles, Washington, D.C., Boston, Philadelphia, and St. Louis experimented with some form of school decentralization. Chicago and Dallas sought different types of management reform efforts to "beat the bureaucracy."

Soon after Harvey Scribner was selected as the new chancellor of the New York City school system in 1970, he began talking about restructuring the bureaucracy. To some it might have seemed that the decentralization efforts of 1968–1969 would have accomplished just that, but reorganization has always had a continuing vitality. And, in fact, despite the decentralization of the elementary and junior high schools in New York City, the high schools and certain special schools were placed under the central Board of Education. In addition, many support functions such as payroll, purchasing and supplies, school maintenance and building, and curriculum design remained the responsibilities of the central Board. According to the modified budget of the New York City Board of Education for 1970–1971, the first year after decentralization, 27,303 full-time positions, in addition to quite a few hourly and per diem positions, remained under the central Board, not including positions supported by state and federal funding.

Scribner's commitment to "beating the bureaucracy" had contributed to his acceptance by the New York City Board of Education as the decentralized system's first chancellor. Like Scribner himself, all but two of the members of the Board of Education were new to the system. Scribner often expressed his suspicions of those who had preceded him in the New York City system, and he denigrated those who now ran the system. His remark to one of the senior officials in the system expressed his view of himself as an antibureaucrat: "Jack, you're the perfect bureaucrat. Guys like you never get things done." Moreover, writing in the *New York Times* Educational Supplement, in January 1971, Scribner declared: "Reform in the 1970s ought to be directed at the structures and system of education."

Quick to join in condemnation of excessive bureaucracy, Scribner was a ready follower of the trend of the early 1970s to emphasize management reform in education. Management reform became another dimension of "beating the bureaucracy." In early 1971, Scribner agreed to accompany a private consulting firm to Albany to seek $300,000 from the State Education Department for a year-long review of management of the New York City school system. When the trip was unsuccessful, Scribner began discussions with the Economic Development Council (EDC), a consortium of large New York corporations, which lent executives for public service and eventually undertook a major management study of the New York City Board of Education.

But New York City had no monopoly on its desire to reform

the bureaucracy through more effective management. In May 1967, a major management survey was presented to the Board of Education of the city of Chicago and it was adopted, in February 1968, as the basis for major reform efforts. Dallas Superintendent Noland Estes, during the 1970s, established a reputation as a management reformer. Indeed, bureaucratic reorganization was a continuing theme as school systems throughout the country were reorganized and new management systems installed.

Efforts at bureaucratic reform were a major focus of the efforts of big city systems during the 1960s and 1970s. Whether these changes focused on administrative decentralization, community control, or management reform, they all hoped to remake the educational bureaucracy and make it "accountable" and "responsive," two key words of those days. Indeed, it seemed as if the one issue everyone could agree upon was the need for reform in big city education. Yet, the more outspoken parents, both proponents of integration and segregation, the teachers and administrators, and the outside business community often meant different things by their criticism of "big" bureaucracy. And was bureaucracy really beatable? Or were diverse interests merely couching their particularistic demands in deliberately vague language that tended to obscure their own interests? Finally, to what extent were bureaucratic reform efforts a part of the larger contest among competing social, ethnic, and racial groups for control over the educational system?

Establishing the Big City School System

The demand for bureaucratic reform, which expressed itself during the 1960s and 1970s in large city school systems, was a replay of a theme recurrent throughout the twentieth century. The unification of large city school systems during the early part of the century was promoted in the interests of greater efficiency in emulation of the successful large business corporation. Later, Frederick W. Taylor popularized scientific management principles, which became the basis for the further advocacy of the efficiency criterion in education as well as other public and private organizations. Business executives, gaining ascendancy in American life and on boards of education, asserted that the schools could be run more efficiently, and that private business organizations should be used as models for the schools. The contextual elements of the 1960s and 1970s were similar to those of the 1910s and 1920s.

The nineteenth century saw the ascendancy of business managers and entrepreneurs to positions of leadership in America. Their success in amassing personal fortunes gave credence to their claims of organizational expertise. Business and the success of business dominated American culture at the turn of the century. At the same time, the waves of immigration during the nineteenth century, together with the American tradition of local control, resulted in the assumption of political power by new immigrant groups in large cities. Attempts by school leaders, during the nineteenth century, to create smooth-running, rational, conflict-free bureaucracies were met, therefore, with opposition from these groups. They questioned the basic purposes and conduct of public education, fighting the crude assimilationist view they sometimes encountered. They fought the creation of impersonal systems, unable to respond to the problems of their individual heritages and ethnic differences. For the newer Americans, ethnic diversity and political competition eclipsed the drive for more rational management techniques.

But to professional educators of the time, the imperatives of a centralized system, run by professionals, were

extraordinarily appealing. Political conflict and lay control
were viewed as contrary to their own rational pursuit of
system goals. A centralized system run by a professional
hierarchy, they argued, meant the regularization of routines
and maximization of their own control over a rational
bureaucracy.

Conflict was particularly acute over the school system,
even exceeding that in other spheres of public activity.
Since the earlier acceptance of the principle of free public
elementary education, public resources devoted to
education were substantial. Furthermore, the schools
constituted a major point of contact with the immigrant
populations. A survey by the United States Senate
Immigration Commission, for example, indicated that in
37 of the largest cities in the country, children of more than
60 nationalities could be counted, and over 58 percent of
all students were the children of fathers born abroad. The
problems of integrating these students into American life
were soon recognized as pervasive.

But the conflict among ethnic groups that expressed
itself in the schools was merely a part of a larger social
phenomenon, in which new ethnic groups were seeking
access to the processes of influence and power in America.
Education, which seemed to these immigrants to offer
their children success, became a focal point for the broader
social and political struggle. Aroused, ethnic groups began
quarreling over bilingualism, as well as ethnic references
in the curricula and their own sense of identity. These
groups also met resistance from the white Protestant groups
who were losing political control in the cities. School
systems at the turn of the century, in large cities, tended to
be in the hands of local boards and ward leaders specific to
each neighborhood. In the decentralized school system,
corresponding to the overall decentralized political system,

new ethnic groups found themselves more and more in
control. In the 28 cities with a population of 100,000 or more,
there were 603 central board members—an average of 21.5
per city. In addition, there were hundreds of ward school
board members in some of the largest cities. By 1913, these
same cities had only 264 board members for an average of
10.2, while ward boards had all but disappeared.

These changes in the number of school boards reflected
the movement toward centralization then sweeping large
city education. School professionals, seeking to minimize
lay intervention and control, encouraged centralized school
administration. Their claim of greater efficiency in
large-scale and professional organization, with its
concurrent bureaucratization of the school system, was
consistent with the dominant corporate model of large-scale
organizations. The new professionals willingly adopted the
business model in an era when the success of the business
elite was an accepted premise of American life. The
creation of centralized educational bureaucracies on the
corporate model brought together the interests and
concepts of the powerful business elite and the educational
professionals.

A centralized corporate model, however, was just the
beginning. Concurrent with the unification of large city
school systems, other efficiency criteria began to be
applied. As early as 1911, just as the final installment of
Frederick W. Taylor's widely publicized series in *American
Magazine* was appearing, Simon Patten, a well-known
economist and reformer, demanded that schools
demonstrate their contribution to society or face budget
cuts. In a follow-up article entitled "An Economic Measure
of School Efficiency," Patten challenged educators to
demonstrate results that could be seen and measured.

The educational profession was quick to repond to

criticisms of school efficiency, sensing perhaps that scientific management might be a key to a greater recognition of their own professional status. At the annual meeting of the National Education Association, a committee was constituted to study tests and the standards of efficiency of schools and school systems. Also, in 1911, the High School Teachers Association of New York City began a three-year study of efficiency in the high schools, applying the principles of scientific management. During the next decade, educational administrators responded vigorously to the demands for greater efficiency. They then applied the principles of scientific management to classroom learning. They sought to reorganize both schools and school systems. Efficiency bureaus, with staffs of efficiency experts, sprang up in large cities and prominent professors of educational administration became consultants for a fee. Then, too, centralization of large city school systems was followed by the consolidation of smaller rural districts, a process which continues. Management reform efforts, often improving upon the crude examples, which Raymond Callahan cites in the *Cult of Efficiency,* have been institutionalized in periodic school surveys by professional educators and management consultants.

During the 1960s, however, two conflicting forces came to challenge the consensus over central control of big city education. On the one hand, teachers became increasingly better organized, and unions began to be recognized as collective bargaining agents in the big cities. On the other hand, the newer ethnic groups emerging in the large cities —the blacks and the Hispanics—began to demand greater control over the educational system. Both these groups sought to beat the centralized bureaucracy, though they often meant different things by the slogans they used in common.

The Growth of Teacher Unionism

The movement toward the centralized system, which dominated big city education during the first half of the twentieth century, had the consequence of increasing the bureaucratization of the school system. Larger school systems meant larger central staffs, the proliferation of nonteaching personnel, and the depersonalization of the educational process. The distance between central administrators and teachers working in the classroom increased. At the school level, the notion of the principal as principal teacher, deriving legitimacy from the teaching staff, was no longer applicable, if in fact it had ever existed. The principal was now selected by a central group headed by a city-wide superintendent. To the typical classroom teacher, these changes were interpreted as part of a headquarters establishment, which was at best unfathomable and at worst bent on the dehumanization and exploitation of the teacher.

Teachers' feelings of powerlessness and estrangement provided an important base upon which union leaders could organize during the 1960s. While the degree of bureaucratization varied among schools, James Anderson, in *Bureaucracy in Education,* discussed the pervasiveness of this phenomenon within several schools in one large metropolitan school district. He noted that "more and more teachers identify school administrators with the bureaucratic structure, its centralization of authority and rigid prescription of behavior."

During that decade, particularly in large cities, the American Federation of Teachers (AFT) and the National Education Association (NEA) began a rapid development, based in considerable part upon the feelings of alienation that had developed during the centralization and bureaucratization of large city school systems. The creation of large school systems, with so many teachers sharing common problems, however, had helped form a critical mass feeding the remarkable growth of these two national organizations. They were helped, too, by the public attitude toward collective bargaining, shaped in part by the path-breaking executive actions of Mayor Robert Wagner of New York City and President John F. Kennedy, supporting the right of public employees to participate in collective bargaining.

As teacher unionism grew, the classroom teachers' militancy grew—and their desire for union power. In a survey of union leaders conducted during the 1960s, Alan Rosenthal found the widespread belief that teachers experienced almost no control over educational policy, with the exception of salary and related matters where they had an extremely limited voice. These leaders saw the need for teachers' organizations to gain power over general policy, salary policy, school organization, personnel policy, curriculum and instruction.

While the growth of teacher organizations may be seen as a response to the growth of the centralized bureaucracies that provided educational services, they came to be viewed by others as an integral part of the professional monopoly over education that excluded public control.

By the late 1960s, many of the advocates of decentralization saw it as a strategy to reduce the power of city-wide unions, which had formed close relationships with central headquarters. In fact, by 1970, when Chancellor Harvey Scribner took office in New York City, his own fears of bureaucratization extended to the teachers union. Expressing the desire to abridge the power of the teachers union and its leader Albert Shanker, he championed decentralization against the centralized, city-wide power

of the union. In the never-never world of educational
reorganization, within a ten-year period, the teachers
union—which had long advocated decentralization as a
remedy to an unresponsive headquarters staff—was now
advocating greater power for the central board of education,
while the city schools chancellor—normally in favor of
enhanced centralization—sought decentralization—in part
to reduce the city-wide power of the union.

The resulting conflict between Shanker and Scribner was
dramatic evidence of the power of the teachers union. It
would be an oversimplification to view the fall of Scribner as
a Shanker victory, yet the very level of the conflict suggests
that teachers in the 1970s had risen to a position of power
far exceeding earlier expectations.

Teachers unions in other cities looked to New York as a
leading example of what teacher power could mean and
recognized its skillful use and manipulation by electing
Albert Shanker president of the AFT.

By the early 1970s, teachers unions in most major cities
not only had enlisted large followings, but were exercising
increasing power in city politics. They had learned to cope
with big city educational systems by organizing on a big
scale. They provided teachers with a measure of control and
increasing political power. Some indication of the progress
they had made as political organizations can be seen
by the fact that both national teacher organizations, the
AFT and the NEA, endorsed Jimmy Carter's presidential
candidacy in 1976, thus breaking a long tradition of not
endorsing candidates for national office. The organized
teachers, in the 1970s, were becoming increasingly
comfortable with their new political role.

The rise of teacher unionism and teacher power during
the 1960s and 1970s must be seen from another perspective,
too. As the new minorities began to enter the public
schools in increasing numbers, and as teachers became

more affluent, the social gap between the teachers and
their students increased. Moreover, social, ethnic, and racial
differences exacerbated tensions and began to affect the
conflict over power in school systems throughout the
country.

While the demand for decentralization was conceived
initially as a demand for lay control over an increasingly
bureaucratized, professional system, it soon took on an
ethnic and racial dimension. The new ethnic groups, the
blacks and Hispanics, began to view decentralization as a
means of controlling the school system. Control meant
many things, but, most threatingly to the teachers, it meant
jobs. As the underrepresentation of blacks and Hispanics
on teaching and administrative staffs became clearer, the
demands for decentralization as a remedy for this imbalance
posed a direct threat to the white teachers. Matters of
power vis-à-vis the central administration were subordinated
as city-wide teacher organizations became more successful
in dealing with city boards of education. A new alliance of
professionals of similar ethnic and social backgrounds
now formed and solidified against the demands for
decentralization of the bureaucracy. Decentralization's
threat to professional and social-class domination mobilized
those who now sought to preserve the centralized system.

Moves Toward Decentralization

It was now left to the new minorities to espouse
decentralization. Many soon forgot the roots of the
decentralization efforts as a reaction to the
bureaucratization of the large city school systems. Yet these
roots affected the controversy. Professor Paul Mort, of
Teachers College at Columbia University, had begun a
series of studies, which were continued by his students

during the 1940s, postulating that local support and local initiative were lacking in large city school systems. In fact, these studies and the concerns they raised finally led to the creation of the Bronx Park Community Project, during the late 1950s, to test the advantages of local control within a large city school system. This project was the forerunner of the community school movement as exemplified by Ocean Hill–Brownsville in New York City and the Adams–Morgan School in Washington, D.C.

A survey conducted in the early 1970s indicated that, of the twenty largest school systems in the United States, only three reported no plans for decentralization. While the responses of the school systems in the survey may be somewhat exaggerated, they indicate a striking acceptance of administrative decentralization. School officials in those years wished to portray themselves as engaging in the trend toward decentralized administration so favorably viewed by the larger professional and lay public.

Implementation of administrative decentralization did not, however, put an end to demands for bureaucratic reform. The concept of community control, or the fracturing of larger school districts into even smaller, autonomous ones, became a rallying cry of the late 1960s in Los Angeles, Detroit, and New York City. But decentralization of large city school systems, which had slowly begun to develop a constituency among teachers and parents of all ethnic backgrounds, became transformed into an ethnically divisive issue. Decentralization became the program of the new black and Hispanic ethnic groups as a way of increasing their control of and power over education at the expense of the previously dominant whites. Primarily-white teachers unions suddenly found themselves in direct opposition to the demands of many influential black and Hispanic groups. These issues, considered elsewhere at great length, demonstrate vividly how abstractions, such as

ideal school district size and administrative efficiency, can
become subordinate to the realities of group conflict.

Management Reform

In an earlier era, centralization efforts gave way to other
management reforms often associated with scientific
management. During the 1960s and early 1970s,
decentralization, too, gave way to the search for
management reforms. While earlier management reform
efforts had been a technique for reasserting centralized
control, they were now viewed as consistent with the
principles of decentralization.

Chicago, New York City, and Los Angeles were cities
that during this same period of decentralization sought to
reform from above by calling in management groups to
assess the functioning of the centralized operations.
Management reforms sometimes involved management
studies. In other cases, they called for new management
systems such as the Planning, Programming, Budgeting
Systems (PPBS), Management by Objectives (MBO), or
Management Information Systems (MIS). On other occasions,
they involved more limited endeavors, such as the adoption
of specific techniques like Operations Research, Critical
Path Method, or Project Management.

Comprehensive school management was perhaps most
heavily influenced during the 1960s and 1970s by the
movement to introduce program budgets into the education
area. The letters PPBS became familiar to school personnel
across the country as Planning, Programming, Budgeting
Systems were proposed for major school systems.
Organizations like the Stanford Research Institute, the
Rand Corporation, and Riverside Research, which had been
instrumental in the previous Department of Defense efforts

to introduce PPBS, began working with school districts. Much of the impetus for the application of PPBS to the public sector thus arose from Defense Secretary Robert McNamara's efforts to introduce PPBS in the Department of Defense. McNamara, who had been chief executive officer of the Ford Motor Company, had developed PPBS as a method of assessing competing approaches to national security, including weapons systems.

Later acting at McNamara's urging, President Lyndon Johnson attempted to implement PPBS throughout the federal government. Meanwhile, efforts were also being made to implement PPBS in state and local agencies. In 1966, the Ford Foundation sponsored such an effort, which involved five states, five counties, and five cities. Publications in 1967 and 1968 promoted PPBS for wider dissemination in state and local governments and school systems.

By 1971, a PPBS project, cooperatively managed by the Research Corporation of the Association of School Business Officials and Dade County Public Schools, had been completed. This project included pilot testing of program budget concepts and techniques in school districts across the country: Clark County (Las Vegas), Nevada; Douglas County, Colorado; Herricks and New Hyde Park, New York; Memphis, Tennessee; Milwaukee, Wisconsin; Montgomery County, Maryland; Peoria, Illinois; and Westport, Connecticut. During the late 1960s, other school districts, including Baltimore, Chicago, Los Angeles, Memphis, New York, Philadelphia, Sacramento, Skokie, and Pearl River (N.Y.), had introduced forms of program budgeting. Efforts to disseminate PPBS included periodic workshops at New York University, run by Professor Harry Hartley, as well as publications by the National Academy for School Executives and the United States Office of Education as reflected in its revision of *Financial Accounting,* which stresses program budgeting concepts. By the end of the 1970s, it looked as if

PPBS had peaked and was giving way to other management approaches.

Yet the lesson of New York City's failure with PPBS is instructive. Just as PPBS was getting off the ground, the New York City school system began to deal with the decentralization issue. PPBS was lost amid the pleas of the professionals for less onerous and more useful management approaches and shunted aside by the more telling issues of decentralization and community control. Although the potential of budgeting reform for bringing resource allocation to public view was never fully explored, the demand for citizen control and the struggle for power among ethnic groups of the late sixties quickly eclipsed PPBS.

Similarly, across the country, PPBS ran into a multitude of problems. Aside from the problems of implementing such a system in the area of education and the resistance of the professionals who expected little payback for their efforts, it did not direct itself to the social and racial conflicts that dominated public education.

As the impetus toward PPBS began to fade toward the beginning of the 1970s, a new management approach gained currency. This approach may be broadly characterized as Management by Objectives (MBO) or Performance Planning. MBO was clearly derived from the private sector, where it was quite popular during the 1950s and 1960s. Pioneered by such individuals as Peter F. Drucker and Douglas McGregor, MBO stood for a more participative style of management, incorporating specifically agreed upon performance objectives. While MBO has been generally hailed as successful in business enterprises, the results of systematic evaluations are more tentative. Nonetheless, it became quite popular as yet another business-oriented approach that promised success for educational management.

A survey, which was conducted in the fall of 1974, indicated that close to 50 systems in the country had experimented with MBO or Performance Planning. Among these were 10 large city school districts, Pittsburgh, Cincinnati, Detroit, Miami, Dallas, Chicago, Los Angeles, San Francisco, Oakland, and San Diego. Yet only the Pittsburgh program seemed viable, and that had only begun the previous summer. Of the 20 smaller schools, listed as having implemented a system of evaluation by objectives in a survey prepared by George Redfern of the American Association of School Administrators in April 1973, at least 7 had dropped the system by the following fall.

In analyzing the failure of Performance Planning systems to take hold in large city school systems, several factors can be cited. In many cases, the new methods did not receive the full support of the top management in the school system. In others, supervisors could not be persuaded to go along. In still others, the unions undermined MBO. The difficulties of defining performance objectives in a school setting stumped others. Yet, underlying all these specific reasons was a more basic reality. Despite the problems confronting the large city school systems, performance objectives and their implementation were a luxury that could not be afforded. As attention was directed toward more immediate problems of values and conflicts among ethnic groups, the comparative luxury of management reform became secondary.

During the 1960s and 1970s, the conflict over values dominated the politics of the schools. Where a particularly able administrator like Noland Estes of Dallas believed in a management system and devoted energy to it, it could work. But even the efforts of a dedicated superintendent did not mean much where racial and social conflict was strong.

Management reforms such as Performance Planning,

which threatened to alter the incentive structure and provide competitive monetary rewards, also ran against the current of teacher unionism, which sought uniformity of treatment. The demand, in a time of social conflict, for open systems of evaluation made MBO even more objectionable to school staffs. In the end, staff members did not accept such reforms—as the earlier professionals had—but fought the changes and redirected their efforts to teacher unionism.

Toward the middle of the 1970s, the attention that had been focused on PPBS and MBO earlier began broadening to include the systems approach. Often PPBS and MBO were included in this general approach to management, which, according to the skills of its developer, was more or less sensitive to the problems of education. By this time, operations research, organization development, and special techniques such as cost-benefit analysis, Critical Path Method, and Program Evaluation and Review Technique (PERT) were considered legitimate tools of educational managers. The impact of these techniques seemed to be pervasive, and the pressure on administrators to apply business and industrial values and practices to education seemed as cogent in 1970 as Raymond Callahan had observed it to be in 1960.

Callahan was quite pessimistic as to the value of this influence in improving education. He may be read, however, not so much as criticizing the application of management principles to education, but rather as criticizing the overemphasis on them at the expense of the intellectual content of education and educational technique. It may be that the emphasis, in the 1960s and 1970s, on management reform similarly detracted from the solution of the basic social and ethnic conflicts that plagued the schools without end. Those who sought to use management reform as a way of sidestepping the value conflicts that scourged the larger society were disappointed.

From the perspective of the 1970s, perhaps a more optimistic appraisal can be made of the demand for efficiency in education and the application of systematic management principles to it. Certainly, the scale of operations of educational institutions warrants systematic attention to the problems of management. Purchasing and contracting functions are doubtless similar to those operations in other public and private institutions. Goal setting activities by teachers and principals can benefit from insights from other management contexts, as Drucker has pointed out. Perhaps systematic approaches to management will also revolutionize classroom instruction, as is suggested by certain approaches using criterion-referenced tests, which integrate with comprehensive computer-based grading and evaluation systems.

The Economic Development Council— A Case Study

The difficulties that management reform efforts encountered during the 1960s and 1970s are illustrated by the management survey and implementation attempts in New York City undertaken by the EDC.

When Chancellor Harvey Scribner focused upon management reform as a tool for beating the bureaucracy, he decided to ask EDC to undertake a study of the New York City school system. Having recently completed a well-received study of the New York City court system, EDC found the prospect of a major management study of the Board of Education inviting. EDC was a formidable group, founded by George Champion, the former chairman of the

board of directors of Chase Manhattan Bank. Among its
directors were Charles Luce of Consolidated Edison,
Harry Helmsley, the real estate developer, Robert Sarnoff of
RCA, and Gustave Levy from Wall Street.

EDC, in membership and approach, seemed to Harvey
Scribner to offer a breath of new life. But its major
orientation toward "management reform" of public
education, executed in accordance with private business
principles, was merely an updated version of the
management survey, which had been relied on by school
systems throughout the twentieth century.

After several months of private negotiations between the
EDC and the chancellor's office, the EDC task force leader,
on loan from International Business Machines Corporation,
brought together a team of seven additional members,
representing Air Reduction Corporation, General Foods,
Sears, ESSO of New Jersey, Chase Manhattan Bank, Bristol-
Myers, and IBM. For the most part, these men were either at
or near retirement or in the process of career change. For the
most part, too, they were intelligent and interested in public-
sector organizations. They had almost no experience,
however, in public-sector organizations. A good deal of their
time, therefore, was spent in on-the-job learning. Yet, they
did have considerable free time and a mandate from the
chancellor and the Board of Education to undertake a
management survey of headquarters and make suggestions.

On January 11, 1972, Chancellor Scribner sent a memo
to the Board of Education praising the work of the EDC
task force. According to Scribner, the task force had found
that—

1.　large amounts of time were expended on projects of
　　limited impact;
2.　ideas tended to get lost or dissipated;

3. many administrators were untrained and unprepared for the problems that confronted them daily and lacked direct supervision from people who could help them function more effectively;
4. there was a widespread fragmentation of effort.

Their overall conclusions were—

1. that the system as a whole lacked a sense of focus;
2. that the system as a whole required more effective management;
3. that strong central leadership was crucial to the success of decentralization.

EDC's chief recommendation was a major reorganization of the central headquarters that would create four deputy chancellorships, for business and administrative services, for centralized school administration, for community school district relations, and for educational planning and support.

The promulgation of that report was just the beginning of a long series of discussions, sometimes quite heated, among the chancellor, the Board of Education members, and the EDC team. EDC, it soon appeared, was no ordinary consultant. Although unpaid, its members repeatedly exhibited great tenacity and commitment to their own recommendations.

It was not until March 1973 that the Board of Education and the EDC held a joint press conference to announce that a restructured headquarters organization had been agreed upon. After the original proposal had been made, the idea of four new deputy chancellors had been scrapped in the interests of economy, and, in its stead, the existing deputy chancellorship was revised to accommodate the business and administrative functions and three additional executive

directorships were created for centralized school
administration, community school district affairs, and
educational planning and support.

The chairman of the EDC task force pointed out that the
study had utilized 22 work-years by "on-loan" executives
from 15 contributing companies—with an estimated value
of $600,000. George Champion suggested,

> This is the first major step on the road to the more
> efficient and effective organization and operation of our
> City's school system. . . . EDC welcomes this opportunity
> to help apply the tools of the improved development of
> modern management to the all-important task of public
> education. . . .

Such a statement could easily have been made by the
proponents of Frederick W. Taylor's scientific management
in the 1920s.

The press release announcing the reorganization also
mentioned that final interviews for the executive
directorships would take place immediately, and that an
extensive search had been undertaken for candidates to
fill these positions. Even so, the atmosphere of cooperation
that characterized the press conference soon deteriorated,
as the EDC task force found their recommendations ignored
in the selection of top executives. Soon after the
reorganization was announced, in late April of 1973,
Scribner resigned (for other reasons, which will be
discussed later). EDC wrote to the Board of Education that,
unless their suggestions for a replacement were taken
seriously, the task force would withdraw. At one point, a
"yelling and banging" match took place between EDC and
the president of the Board of Education, with the latter
calling the EDC plan "sophomoric and shoddy." The Board

of Education privately agreed later, too, that EDC could go
if it wished.

It did not, and in October 1973, the EDC task force
chairman warned the Board not to make its projected
appointments for deputy chancellor and executive director
of personnel. EDC wrote:

> We have been most patient in our understandings of the
> multiple situations that occupy your Board's time. But, if
> our work is to be at all worthwhile, we just cannot operate
> on the basis of disregard of our judgment. Ask yourself
> the question will [the Board] live up to the scope of its
> responsibility if this and further major executive
> appointments are made as has your recent Chancellor
> selection without seeking the most qualified person
> available. . . .

The Board had gone along with the EDC reorganization
proposal as revised, but refused to accept the EDC
recommendations for major posts under the new
organization.

In the words of one school professional who had seen
reorganization before, "Nothing's changed and no one's
doing anything differently." But changes were made, at
least in the staff at the top level. The former deputy
chancellor, Irving Anker, became the first Jewish permanent
head of the New York City school system, after long years
of service. Bernard Gifford, a young black, former head of
the New York City Rand Corporation became deputy
chancellor. Frank Arricale, a politically active Italo-
American, became executive director of personnel. Edythe
Gaines, the most prominent black woman in the New York
City school system, was promoted to executive director
for planning and support. Alfredo Mathews, Jr., the most

prominent Hispanic in the school system, was appointed executive director for community school district affairs. Samuel Polatnick, Jewish, a longtime high school principal, became executive director of the high schools and Helen Donovan Feulner, Irish-Catholic, another longtime toiler in the New York City schools, became executive director of special schools.

In the end, smarting perhaps over their going outside the system in their selection of Scribner—who was in retrospect viewed by Board members as a poor choice—the Board moved back inside the school system. With the exception of Gifford and Arricale, whose ethnic identifications made them particularly attractive, the new team at 110 Livingston Street was composed of seasoned survivors of the bureaucracy.

An Overview

The idea of management reform, which Harvey Scribner had seized upon to bring about "real change" in the bureaucracy, was a convenient, but unsuccessful strategy. Scribner, the WASP reformer, whose ethnic credentials actually made him the ideal mediator between New York's ethnic groups—the Jews, the Irish, the Italians—and the newer ethnic groups—the blacks and Hispanics—slipped unknowingly into the strategy of his forebears. With more inspired leadership, such as that offered by Noland Estes in Dallas, he might have made management reform work. With more forceful and effective politics, such as Superintendent James Redmond had demonstrated in Chicago, he might have been more successful. Yet, in the 1970s, the pleas for reform that had been so successful in earlier days seemed to fall on deaf ears. Even EDC, a group still predominantly Protestant and from the higher levels of management, could not help Harvey Scribner.

Ethnic politics, which EDC could never quite accept, or perhaps did not even understand, was its downfall. At another time in history, major political figures would not have been able to maneuver the power of EDC and its corporate backing into defeat. But, as EDC railed against the ethnic balancing act that characterized the selection of executive directors for the grand reorganization they proposed, the Board of Education moved ahead. The members of the Board were expressing the political imperatives of a system that they understood, mastered, and obeyed, despite the strident voices of the oldest, most established American ethnic group, decrying the current ethnic conflicts and their unwieldy politics of accommodation.

The EDC effort was vulnerable on several fronts. Its emphasis on hierarchy and centralized units ran counter to the decentralization thrust. Its authors had received their training in the hierarchical corporate world, and, in some cases, their formative experiences had occurred in an earlier era. For the most part, though, they were not influenced by the developments in organizational theory of the 1950s and 1960s, stressing the integration of functions, flexibility of organizational structure, and de-emphasizing the need for hierarchy. The greatest irony of the EDC effort, however, was the extent to which ethnic politics, which they sought sometimes to ignore and other times to overcome were ultimately reinforced and strengthened by the personnel selected for the top posts in the EDC reorganization proposal.

Bureaucratic reform took place in every large school system in the country during the 1960s and 1970s. The earlier emphasis on centralization gave way to decentralization. While only Detroit and New York City experienced legislatively mandated decentralization, almost every other major school system experienced administrative decentralization. Management surveys took place in Chicago and New York City as well as a host of other cities. PPBS, MBO, and MIS were tried throughout the country with only mild success. Yet, to a remarkable degree, these bureaucratic reforms reflected and were influenced by the dynamics of ethnic, racial, and social conflict that were affecting big city education. As these tensions are muted during the coming decade, the attempt by administrators to implement these approaches will become increasingly successful. And, as these reforms become better adapted to the circumstances of public education, they promise to form a more important and more effective tool for school managers.

Bureaucratic reform in school systems, just as in business organizations, can lead to greater effectiveness and efficiency. Management reform was a successful strategy in some instances, but the conflict among ethnic groups was by far the more compelling issue. Management reform illustrates as poignantly as some other issues do the pervasive impact of ethnic and social conflict on public education during the 1960s and early 1970s. In much the same way as reform of local governmental institutions at the turn of the century reflected the conflict of ethnic groups for political control, bureaucratic reform of educational systems during the 1960s and 1970s mirrored current group conflicts. The allocation of resources among competing groups was the higher priority issue in the large cities during this period.

"Beating the bureaucracy" will undoubtedly continue to be an issue in the future of American public education. Americans are great reformers and reform will continue to

concern the American educational community. As the
conflicts of the 1970s subside, bureaucratic reform will
become more successful as a strategy. It will become less
a method for beating the bureaucracy than for reinforcing
the claims of the professional educators themselves to
expertise and legitimacy.

Changing the Way Education Is

Bureaucratic reform often draws upon the larger reservoir of sentiment for educational change. Since the late 1950s, a small band of intellectuals has been insisting—often incisively and correctly—that American schoolrooms are typically boring, alienating, repressive, and stifling. By the 1960s, increasingly large numbers of educational professionals, including teachers and administrators, began to agree, as did parents and their children. Soon the air was filled with talk of "irrelevant" education and its undefined reverse, "relevance"; of "change" and "change agents"; of "de-schooling" and "informal schools." By the early 1970s, the themes of Paul Goodman, George Leonard, Ivan Illich, John Holt, Jonathan Kozol, Herbert Kohl, and others became a "movement," and after them came their adherents and practitioners.

At first, conventional educators reacted against this movement, feeling threatened and confused by the assault on their values and teaching techniques. For many of them, the best schooling was embodied in standard lesson plans, mass testing, learning-by-rote, so-called basic learning-without-thinking ("name three causes of the French Revolution"), and the absence of moral reasoning and ethical alternatives. Even so, in cities such as Philadelphia, San Francisco, and Dallas, school superintendents helped introduce important modifications. The Parkway School in Philadelphia, for example, occupied an abandoned elementary school building and populated it with concerned and interested teachers who volunteered to work with the students who chose to study there. Mark Shedd, the superintendent, lent the force of his office to Parkway School. Such innovations were less threatening to teaching staffs than statements such as those made by Ewald B. Nyquist, New York State's Commissioner of Education who said, in December 1970: "Our present system of public education, coercive in its methods, is a symptom and a major cause of our unsatisfactory way of life." And he was echoed repeatedly by New York City's first schools chancellor, Harvey B. Scribner. Big city schools, he said, were "in serious trouble" with a dismal "record of academic failure." The most telling criticism of those years came with the publication of the Carnegie Foundation's three-and-one-half-year study of American education, *Crisis in the Classroom,* in which the study's director Charles Silberman charged that schools were "joyless" and "mindless."

"Reform" was suddenly acceptable. Everywhere "experimental" schools were developed. Some, like John

Dewey High School in New York City, Village School in Great Neck, New York, and John Adams High School in Portland, Oregon, were organized with care, planning, and support from the central staff and faculty unions. But such successful ventures were rare in terms of their staying power and the quality of education offered. In addition, these schools catered essentially (but not entirely) to white middle-class students. Where efforts were made to reach out to poor nonwhite students the results were as bleak as in the conventional schools.

The New Jersey Street Academies were initiated, in April 1968, by Governor Richard J. Hughes to try to help those estranged from traditional schools. By July, the street academies received $460,000 for their first year of operation. Special resources were offered; several state agencies were ordered to cooperate; staff was hired. "Few programs have begun more auspiciously," wrote two evaluators of the program. Yet soon afterward, the critics continued, the schools became "an administrative and fiscal monstrosity," replete with well-paid but less than helpful consultants, endless meetings, shoddy controls, little planning or teacher training, and little understanding of what alternative schooling was all about.

Even so, although most of the reformers' pet projects failed, their basic criticisms of traditional schools cannot easily be dismissed. At the heart of much of the criticism of the best of the reformers was the desire to encourage more openness in students and their greater responsibility for their own learning, with the teacher as intellectual guide rather than authoritarian figure, and a wish to heighten moral sensibilities. But few students had the self-discipline or wherewithal to take on so weighty a responsibility. Only a small number of teachers were willing or able to forgo their customary roles as the dominant presence in the classroom. Typically, too many administrators and parents said,

"Innovate all you want, so long as you don't change anything." And too many reformers-in-office equated reform with civil war against their teaching staffs. Some, as in New York City, tended to side exclusively with black interests, as opposed to white ethnics, in their zeal to redress the customary imbalance of educational priorities.

Still, reform—however defined—was a worthy goal for those who believed education was more than formal instruction, homework, unquestioning obedience to authority, and passive acceptance of conventional wisdom. Experimentation and innovation became the reformers' battle cry. True, they often sounded like the progressive educators of the 1920s and 1930s. Yet many had a resiliency and influence unknown to the followers of John Dewey. They were more individualistic for one thing, more daring in their ideas, less trusting of government, more damning of the status quo. The early and original critics (Goodman, Leonard, Kozol) wrote of humanistic values and compassion for the poor and nonwhites. But, as with Dewey's pioneering work, many of their followers did not understand the pioneers or misapplied their teachings, if indeed they ever understood them. For many of the followers it was enough to speak or write about contemporary school problems or at best try to wish them away with compassion. But, for the students who desperately needed help, warm wishes were not enough.

Nowhere was this more evident than in the Philadelphia public schools. There Mark Shedd, a handsome, articulate, and reform-minded superintendent of schools, tried to institute change in the system. Shedd brought with him a vast store of ideas, a large and dedicated staff of bright young men and women, and great hopes. It was a kind of social revolution undertaken by an elite sitting in offices at a remote central headquarters.

If there was a reform or innovation conceived anywhere

during the late 1960s and early 1970s, it was probably
considered or implemented in Philadelphia. The Parkway
School, the first "school without walls" in the country,
began there. Shedd also brought the prestigious North
Carolina Advancement School to his city, hoping that it
would become a "major agent of change." Teachers and
principals were offered special incentive funds—as high as
$15,000 a year for principals and up to $3,000 for teachers
—for their special projects. Sensitivity retreats were
arranged, unofficial "ombudsmen" established, black
organizations welcomed into the schools, storefront and
community schools encouraged, and a "talent pool" of
teachers developed from which principals might staff their
schools.

Henry Resnick, in *Turning On the System: War in the
Philadelphia Public Schools,* discussed many of these
changes and, despite his apparent sympathies for Shedd
and his staff, concluded that the Shedd revolution failed.
The old bureaucracy went its own way, at best oblivious to
the turmoil in the schools and at worst thoroughly
disgusted with Shedd and his aides. There was no
administrative reorganization to accompany educational
reforms. "The changes at the top and the bottom are not
as important as those at the middle, for it's the middle
managers who can kill you," said one knowledgeable New
York bureaucrat. As the sociologist Max Weber has observed,
"The question is always who controls the existing
bureaucratic machinery." And, in Philadelphia, headquarters
and school staffs resented being told, albeit implicitly, that
they had failed and that *they*—and not the city's monumental
problems relating to poverty and white flight—were at fault.
This, at least, is the way they interpreted the revolution. At
the same time, Shedd moved to open up administrative
ranks to blacks and sympathetic whites. He did so swiftly

and savagely, for he was permitted to make 5 percent of his administrative appointments outside civil service requirements. In retrospect, he cleaned out some featherbedders and opened up many significant posts to black teachers and supervisors. Yet, could these gains have been accomplished more humanely? Might it not have been possible to encourage early retirement or to add staff without firing indiscriminately? And, perhaps most significantly, to what extent did these changes promote learning in the classroom?

Even the Advancement School had a "negative effect." Its students "returned to their home schools even more hostile to traditional teaching methods than they had been before. They had glimpsed the future; they had tasted freedom." Said one student: "They turned me on! Then they put me back and let me get turned off again!"

In the end, many people drew back, frightened by the implications of swift change. One always needs to prepare carefully for any radical departure from established policy. And one needs to not only explain carefully changing policies and their implications to the public but also reassure all those with legitimate interests and to stress their stakes in the new programs. Then the debate begins. These steps Shedd failed to take. "Shedd's talented central staff continued to make the big decisions, and with so much creative thinking going on in the top administration, the system was in some ways even more centralized than before," wrote Resnick.

Moreover, in reality, Shedd's most radical ideas were hardly revolutionary, but they were generally harbingers of things to come across the nation. But, lacking a firm base of support at headquarters and among his professional staff, beset by a divided, lay board of education and an unsympathetic City Hall, confronted by whites deeply

resentful of "concessions" to blacks, and facing the
desperate problems of the expanding black ghettos,
Shedd's program was not successful. Philadelphia
youngsters in both the new and the traditional schools did
no better than pupils in comparable urban school systems
elsewhere.

In early 1965, Martin Mayer, member of a Manhattan
local school board and a journalist, warned of deteriorating
conditions in the New York public schools. He wrote of the
"narrow bitterness" that permeates school politics, of the
"road most Negro and Puerto Rican children are traveling
. . . [leading] . . . only to unskilled manual labor or the
gutter," and of school administrators "like the former
Chinese gentry . . . ranked in a rigid hierarchy of status,
achieved through the passage of examinations which fail
to measure either the intellectual or temperamental qualities
needed for the job."

More than a decade later, it is very difficult to judge how
much has changed. What remains is the terrible sense of
urgency felt in the city's classrooms by many parents and
teachers. Reading failures remain extraordinarily high and
average daily attendance is one of the lowest in the
country.

In those years, too, millions of words of withering prose,
on the mark, but also overblown and oversimple and vague,
had been published.

The fault of the new educational critics lay precisely in
their ambiguity and intellectual sloppiness. They ignored
reality. They mercilessly castigated the teacher. They
offered no way of measuring student accountability. They
had few educational goals and fewer still that were
attainable, even if desirable. A perceptive critic, Arthur
Pearl, wrote: "The teacher is postulated to be a part of a
process designed to produce enormous change, yet he is

without even a map specifying *where he is and where he is trying to go."* He continued:

There is a romantic, recurring notion that powerful and valid criticism of existing conditions automatically leads to relief from those conditions. Persons who hold such a belief stubbornly refuse to learn the lessons of history. The most reasonable and probable result of criticism without a defensible alternative is a change that really is no change.

With no goals, no theory, no strategy for a broad change, no political tactics, and, too often, no important allies, most of the new critics found themselves isolated, unable to offer any important and practical help to big city schools.

In general, concluded Pearl, "postulating advanced radical goals and posturing about them is less than useful. We don't need a lot of rhetoric about change; rather, we need lots more education and politics—persuasion of people through everyday processes."

Yet, what was worth pursuing was just that "education and politics and persuasion." Furthermore, experience had shown that the benefits from programs which were added on—however beneficial—in the sense that men, money, and materials were superimposed from the outside, faded away as soon as the outside support was withdrawn.

Educational reform was in the air in New York City in the late 1960s and early 1970s. Despite its reputation as a static leviathan, the New York City school system, in part due to its vast size and in part due to some very creative employees, had an amazing variety of educational programs that had begun and were nurtured in its schools. Higher Horizons was the prototype for programs providing enriched opportunities for poor youngsters to move them on to success in college. The More Effective Schools program, included as part of the teachers' union contract, was a model for compensatory education for the poor, and, indeed, served as a pilot for similar programs throughout the country.

So it was not surprising that the new Board of Education, taking office in the spring of 1969 and charged with implementing decentralization, sensed in educational innovation a theme consistent with the new spirit. Educational reform had the added attraction of diverting attention from the endemic ethnic and racial conflict in the schools.

As the New York City Board of Education sought a new head (to be called "Chancellor") for the decentralized school system, the image of an educational leader with new ideas and a reputation for innovation gradually took form. After appointing a low-key and loyal school administrator as acting chancellor, the Board began a nationwide search. This new officer was charged with the control and operation of all senior high schools, city-wide programs, and specialized schools. The chancellor also would be the guardian of the lower schools, with the right to maintain minimum standards and to issue formal orders to the community boards governing these schools.

To the Board members, the future chancellor also represented an opportunity to provide leadership for the beleaguered system. With his authority to set and maintain minimum educational standards, and with a special fund for educational innovation, the chancellor, it was hoped, would be the symbol of and the driving force behind thoroughgoing improvements.

In its initial search the Board of Education was buttressed in these views by McGeorge Bundy, president of the Ford Foundation, and Kenneth B. Clark, the well-known black psychologist and author, both of whom urged the appointment of a tough administrator who could forge a working coalition of outside groups in favor of change. Sargent Shriver and Arthur Goldberg were proposed for the post early on. But, when the name of John Lotz surfaced, this former Board member and Catholic labor official's earlier advocacy of decentralization led Albert Shanker, president of the United Federation of Teachers, to remark that such a selection would not be taken "lying down." When a magazine article, lauding the accomplishments of the superintendent of schools of Tulsa, Oklahoma, appeared, one Board member laughed aloud, "Tulsa has nothing to teach New York." But it was later decided that Vermont, home of Harvey B. Scribner, did.

From the beginning, the Board of Education had all but ruled out educators, seeking instead someone with public relations skills, management expertise, and conflict-resolving ability. At various times, Board members proposed national figures such as John Kenneth Galbraith, the liberal economist, Walter Wriston, president of First National City Bank, Federal Judge Jack Weinstein, Yale's Kingman Brewster, Larry O'Brien, former head of the national Democratic party, Congressman Herman Badillo, Paul Ylvisaker, former Secretary of Defense Robert McNamara, Ralph Bunche of the United Nations, former Attorney General Ramsey Clark, Don Petrie of Avis, and Wilbur Cohen, former Secretary of Health, Education and Welfare.

In May of 1970, almost a year after taking office, the Board of Education finally moved toward making a choice. Of the four finalists, Neil Sullivan, Massachusetts' commissioner of education, Daniel Griffiths, dean of the New York University School of Education, and Harvey B. Scribner, Vermont's commissioner of education, were educators. The fourth, Frederick O'Reilly Hayes, New York City Budget Director, was Mayor Lindsay's choice.

Sullivan never impressed the members of the Board of

Education, and Griffiths eliminated himself after his
declarations against sharing administrative authority with
the members. "I don't want to be the sixth board member,"
he told them. And despite his strong backing from Lindsay—
in fact, perhaps because of it—Hayes came to symbolize
political interference in education. In the end, the most
compelling argument for Scribner was his reputation as an
educational leader and innovator. It was hoped he would
stand a better chance of bringing the school community
together than would Hayes, whose reputation as an
impersonal administrator worked against him.

The long search was at an end. Without ever having
visited Vermont or Teaneck or any other place he had
worked, with only having interviewed a few of the men
and women he had worked for and with, the Board, relying
mainly on its own fallible judgment, and by now tired and
weary of the entire pursuit, accepted the former
superintendent of schools of Teaneck, New Jersey, who was
then State Commissioner of Education of Vermont.

New York City had its first chancellor.

One late-summer Tuesday morning in 1970, Harvey
Scribner came through the revolving doors much earlier
than the members. At 8:45, diffidently, almost humbly, he
walked into the lobby, empty-handed. Slight and balding,
about 5 feet 6 inches tall, fifty-six years old, his sideburns
reaching fashionably to his earlobes and flaring out, a pipe
in his breast pocket (his "security blanket," he would always
tell visitors), he wore a bright green sports jacket and
brown trousers. Looking severe and purposeful, as he
always would to many outsiders, he smiled slightly as he
approached the elevators. He was alone.

"Welcome, Dr. Scribner." The hand-drawn sign was
crudely crayoned in red, white, and blue on a laundry
cardboard and attached with scotch tape to the elevator

car door that moved directly to his suite of offices on the tenth floor.

"That is *one* hick," someone in the lobby giggled. There was talk in the building that he wouldn't last 17 days; it was rumored that a betting pool had already been set up. He quickly introduced himself to an assistant superintendent in the lobby. "Just call me Harvey," the new chancellor said, offering his hand.

Later, not far away, several friends met to discuss the new chancellor. All of them saw themselves as "reformers" and as friends of the new order. All worked at central headquarters. But their subject was less the man than power and its constraints. One of them began.

First, there are the givens: the teachers and supervisors unions. The lack of money, maybe. The bureaucracy's resistance, maybe. The general inertia. The egos. The lack of trust. The constant stream of bullshit by the critics and the defenders. The black versus white crap. The fact that, despite claims by fakers and dreamers, nobody yet knows how to teach enough ghetto kids the three R's. The goddamned size of everything in this town. The fears.

The others chimed in:

Maybe he's got to be like an old ward boss who built his power out of a welter of local interests, who bothered to learn what was pissing people off, who operated from cold, hard facts.

He's got to have a staff, he's got to get organized. He's got to know where he wants to go, his tactics for getting there, to build up allies.

He's got to try to drive a wedge between the teachers and the supervisors.

He has to reach out to the Puerto Ricans and blacks, to the Jews and Italians.

He'll need constituencies, City Hall, and coalitions.

Finally, one of the people, an experienced planner, leaned back and then rose, slowly, ready to leave. "It's a big order. Let's hope this guy can do something."

On two occasions, first at the Barclay Hotel on New York's East Side, on a school holiday in 1970, and afterward, on yet another day off, at the Columbia University Faculty Club, people gathered to lend their support to educational reforms in the city and to give the new chancellor a green light. Scribner and Shanker were there, as were Albert Bowker, City University chancellor, Ewald B. Nyquist, the state commissioner of education, Bayard Rustin, and Blanche Lewis, then head of the United Parents Associations.

By the time of the second meeting, no one seemed to object that Shanker had leaked the story to the *New York Times:* Widespread educational projects were coming, it was reported. Secret meetings had been held. Everyone then turned to the chancellor for leadership. He had been given, within reason, a go-ahead. He had—again, within limits—funds and resources. The state planning unit, located in central headquarters, scheduled a first conference at Teachers College on alternatives and programs available to school districts. The Ford Foundation pledged sympathetic consideration of any proposal submitted, the *Times* dispatch concluded. At the Columbia meeting, Scribner had delivered a vague and somewhat unclear talk. "Does he always ramble that way?" someone asked.

"No, you should hear the brilliant things he's been saying. . . ."

The meeting was over. Nyquist was near the coatroom, talking softly to someone. "That Scribner, he sounds sincere. I think he's shrewd. He might work out."

Toward Educational Alternatives

"Year Two," Scribner told the *Times* at the start of his second year in office, "is the time for some delivery." The major vehicles he chose were more alternative educational programs for high school students and the Learning Cooperative, which was supposed to serve the lower schools. Both were conceived, introduced, and implemented in isolation, at "110," in ways that have serious implications for future reformers.

After preliminary conversations with the Ford Foundation, a decision was reached by Scribner to submit formal proposals. The request for assistance in the high schools was prepared quickly by his staff, following explorations with people involved with alternative schools.

The Learning Cooperative remained an elusive concept. One veteran administrator on his staff was only too willing to advance some concrete ideas. He urged that it be based on general principles—"that parent participation and training be included, staff on all levels involved in the planning and implementation of programs, that effort should be concentrated enough to make a difference and that it be school-based, in order to achieve internal consistency and validity." He also advanced the notion that community school districts be invited to submit proposals and in turn receive assistance. But Scribner could not reach a decision, and dreary meeting followed dreary meeting.

Flying home from Miami Beach, in September 1971, Scribner turned to another aide. "A grand design, that's what I need, one that will reorganize the city's schools. I want you"—and he stopped to view a sketch filled with boxes and arrows he had drawn on the back of the aide's *New Yorker* magazine—"to get moving on this." Charts were prepared, a consultant hired, and the planning staff mobilized. School personnel and students were spoken to and their conclusions noted. A third proposal was prepared by the future director of the Learning Cooperative. Entitled "Reconnection to Learning," almost the exact title of the 1968 Bundy report leading to the demonstration districts, it requested $10 million from the Ford Foundation.

Confronted with three different drafts, Scribner hesitated, then stopped. He couldn't make up his mind.

The so-called alternative high school, developed before Scribner's arrival by the high school office, was the primary method for changing secondary education. Its aim was to give students who were unsuccessful in traditional four-thousand-student high schools, another opportunity to return to the educational mainstream. Everyone appeared to agree that a small setting with supportive services was a hopeful concept.

After several new "alternative" schools were established, an outside organization, the Public Education Association, held a meeting of the teaching staffs, who were enthusiastic. Theirs was a special kind of experiment, the teachers felt, belonging to them and their students—to whom they seemed genuinely devoted. "We are a family," said one teacher. "Somebody cares," said another. "I see this as a peer community," said yet another. "Sometimes I'm the teacher and sometimes not." Local craftsworkers, such as a garage mechanic and a cabinetmaker, and trained street workers would become auxiliary teachers. Three new courses had been developed at one alternative high school and then adopted by the parent school: History of Jazz, Ghetto Politics, and Social Structure of East New York. In another school, students outnumbered faculty on admission committees, one committee passing on new students and the other on new faculty. Overall, the teachers were proud of their newly discovered "tremendous dedication" and innovative impulses, as well as warmed by the acceptance they had gained from previously estranged and largely nonwhite students.

The advantage of concentrating on small alternative schools lay in dealing with the achievable, working with existing schools, personnel, and organizations and focusing first on making better use of existing resources rather than insisting on new resources.

But was the alternative school a practical method of initiating change in the 94 regular New York City high schools? The question is central inasmuch as, throughout the country, school systems turned in those years to the small, generally off-site school as a way of transforming traditional schools, especially for nonwhite youngsters. The problem, however, is that only a minute number of students have been affected in any way by these schools (or street academies, as they are also known).

The more successful private schools, such as Harlem Prep in New York and Sophia House in St. Louis, soon became isolated—straining to remain sufficiently financed and touching the lives of only a handful. They might have been able to carry new ideas back into the public schools and they might even have inspired others within the public schools to develop their own alternatives, but an increasing number of people came to believe that such schools could not have any serious impact on the vast numbers of students unless they themselves became a part of the public system. Whether this is true or not is difficult to determine. It was

accepted, however, as a premise when Scribner ordered
his high school division, in the spring of 1971, to establish
"no less than 10 alternative high schools." At the same time,
three "satellite academies" (also "alternatives") were to be
opened and run jointly by the Board of Education, the
Human Resources Administration, and the City Planning
Commission. They were designed by and in the office of the
chancellor to create programs for career training and
commercial work.

Some of the schools, or programs, inasmuch as they were
expected to become part of schools, did show signs of
hope. The satellite academies were initiated at the top.
The original impetus came from Scribner, wondering aloud
one day at lunchtime what might be done for dropouts in
career education. The issue he raised provided a framework
for examining the Board's plans for career preparation in a
network of comprehensive schools.

Research revealed that, as always, there were serious
problems. The jobless rate for the
sixteen-to-nineteen-year-old age group in the city was
rising sharply. In ghetto areas the 1968 rate was 25.3
percent for the sixteen-to-nineteen-year-olds in contrast
to 6.7 percent for the total population. The economic
recession only aggravated the problem. Scribner also
believed strongly that career education had to be extended
to "general track" students and that any such training
ought to be directed into occupations the City Planning
Commission declared would be badly in need of employees
throughout the seventies, such as the clerical, food,
transportation, electrical and mechanical, computer, and
health trades.

The satellite academies that emerged did at least spell
out their objectives from the start: to reach what Scribner
had once described as "lost youth," those marginal students
who rarely attended school, regularly failed, and hated

whatever might normally have given them tools for their
liberation. The most important goal, then, "becomes the
effective preparation of youth for the world of work. By
such preparation is meant more than skills training . . .
[but, in addition] the individual's self concept—his own
definition of his worth. . . ."

By the spring of 1972, three such academies were
under way. Equally promising was the City as School, once
again illustrative of reforms from the top, having been
initiated by a Board member with full support from the
chancellor and the bureaucracy. The City as School was
just that, a variation on Parkway's school without walls,
but planned from its very inception by students and several
teachers. Funded by the Ford Foundation, and with the
Board promising to accept the school after its planning
stage as a regular high school, it asked only three things of
its faculty: a demonstrated interest in creativity and
educational change, the ability to work collaboratively with
students and to adapt to new professional roles, and a solid
"nuts and bolts" knowledge of outside resources that
could be used effectively during the planning operation.
Ebbets Field School was somewhat similar. It offered still
more alternatives in a conspicuous area, across from 110
Livingston Street, at street level, and visible to passersby.
A variety of programs, from equivalency classes for
dropouts to peer-group leadership programs in narcotics to
programs offering therapy and work-related skills to
schooling for physically handicapped students in
nonsegregated classes, was available.

In New York City, nearly all-black-and-Hispanic
Haaren High School in Manhattan was to be the flagship
of Scribnerian reform. A proposal was developed by the
principal with the help of the New York Urban Coalition,
which saw the school as an opportunity to extend its own
alternative, minischool approach. Almost $250,000 was

collected from two foundations—with the bulk of it coming
from the Ford Foundation. The initial rationale was that
the demand for change was organic, coming from within the
school; and staff, students, and supervisors were to be
involved in the developmental process. On this basis, and
despite the misgivings of his high school division, which
warned privately of the lack of careful planning, the
chancellor moved ahead, pushed by the Urban Coalition
and his own sincere sense of urgency to show results.

The plan, it was revealed later, was conceived and
executed by the principal and a few around him. It was by
no means a genuine outgrowth of the feelings of the staff
and students. It was, instead, an effort to cope with Haaren's
endemic problems, extraordinarily high absentee rates (as
much as 70 percent of the student body were absent),
violence, and official impotence. Hence, Scribner ordered
the project pushed at all costs, and every possible
assistance was offered the school. But, with no adequate
planning (no more than two to three months in extent at
best and then involving very few people), no real preparation
of any kind, the evaluators of the teacher-student summer
institute, which was to redesign the school, concluded that
$100,000 of its initial grant had been wasted.

The purpose of the project was to divide the school
into fourteen smaller schools, such as Basic Skills, Urban
Studies, Aviation, Automobile Mechanics, College Bound,
etc., and to retrain staff while introducing a new
component, the trained streetworker.

The results of Haaren's innovations were confusion of
purpose, unyielding traditionalism on the part of the school
staff and administration, and no measurable improvement
in the quality of education in the classrooms. The only
minischool that "works," the College Bound group, always
has "worked." But, at Haaren, attendance remained as

low as ever, the gap between teachers and students was as great as ever, and the absence of planning is still evident. In 1973, Haaren was the only high school in New York City without an official school newspaper, since it had been closed down by the principal; their only paper was "underground." The assistant superintendent for Manhattan in charge of Haaren, the highest black official in the high school office, reported one semester after it opened, "Haaren was back where Haaren always was," and that "teachers were unprepared for the changes."

Part of the source of the difficulty, in addition to the failure of collaborative planning, is that few persons anywhere had been able to identify the ingredients for success or failure in schools. To "turn everyone loose," as suggested by the chancellor, is hardly an answer, inasmuch as it was difficult to understand what that meant and what everyone was to do once "turned loose." What does emerge at Haaren (which was praised by the *New York Times, Newsweek,* and visiting educators from around the country) is that all such programs, attempting, even theoretically, to initiate serious change, require that—

1. proper preplanning be done in all areas, especially among teachers and administrators.
2. the relationship between staff and students be taken seriously.
3. collaborative planning and development be just that, with all the school's constituents sharing equally.
4. common goals emerge from such joint planning and preparation; they cannot be ordained from headquarters or by the principal.
5. assistance—not control—come from the central staff in supplying the necessary tools.

By the end of its first year, its foundation grants exhausted, none of these requirements had been met at Haaren. The result may have been "A" for effort, but it was "F" for results.

A year before, an effort had been made by the Board's high school office to ask professionals and others "what changes they might like to see." These professionals included the most progressive principals and staff, and the effort resulted in the Task Force on High School Redesign.

The task force's report, "Toward the 21st Century," set forth in twelve pages the "new" strategy to be used in attracting students and teachers. Twelve major reform options, with detailed explanations, were presented as possible remedies. These ranged from an open campus model school, which would function as an all-day (7 A.M. to 10 P.M.) and year-round school, to a "do-it-yourself" or independent study model. The individual suggestions are important in that each idea challenged several existing premises of high schools. Power blocs in the bureaucracy that thrived because of centralization and huge schools and bureaucrats who couldn't move without bureaucratic procedures were challenged by theories that argued for small, 150-pupil schools. The "City as School" and the "School of Municipal Affairs," for instance, conflicted with the idea of the sanctity of the classroom. Here was a major educational report asserting that experience was of equal value to classroom learning. A union that had continually fought for staff-laden projects now had to contemplate a new educational philosophy that might not stress teachers as much as the existing paradigm did. The "Independent Study Model" went a step further, as its students would receive credit for research projects and would not have to attend classes. What is interesting here is the possible conflicts each new suggestion presented to the defenders of the status quo.

A reforming chancellor failed to utilize any part of the report.

Charles Pilgrim, United Parents Associations' new president, the second male and first black ever to run the UPA, sat back and mused. He was an independent middle-of-the-roader who had been against the 1968 teachers strike, and had two children in the public schools. In less than one month, however, on the opening day of school in 1972, the second anniversary of the "reform" administration, he issued a withering blast at Scribner, citing a "crisis in leadership" and adding that "empty promises of reform, of greater parental participation, of curriculum innovation, have been heard far too often to impart any hope."

In addition to the massive problems he had to confront, ethnic politics had also invaded Scribner's domain and complicated his tenure. Privately, Scribner expressed his dismay that most of his opponents were Jewish, although a large number of his supporters were Jewish, too. "In Teaneck [where as superintendent of schools, he had backed school integration] my strongest supporters were Jewish." But a majority of New York City's school supervisors were Jewish, and their class interests dictated opposition to the chancellor who, from the very start of his tenure, lost no opportunity to attack supervisors along with classroom teachers. Later he turned down efforts to meet informally with Polish and Italian groups on the grounds that he was far too busy. In his laudable desire to help nonwhite students, he believed that the way to social justice was to service blacks and Puerto Ricans while ignoring other groups. (It was a blunder made early on by Mayor John V. Lindsay, who remedied his approach in his second term.) Scribner never seemed to recognize the problem. As Joseph Lelyveld argued incisively in the *New York Times,* "New York cares less about what a man

represents than it does about whom he represents.
Scribner represented only his own strong Puritan
conscience; he seeks converts, not allies. In New York that
makes him weak, whatever his position."

When he was forced to resign in the spring of 1973,
Scribner left convinced that ethnic politics had led to his
departure—and in a way they had. He never understood
what made the system work.

The volume of educational reform remained high, but the
effect on student learning was minimal. Despite Scribner's
tendency to introduce reforms from above, he was never
quite at ease with the concept. Indeed, he would
sporadically urge his staff to allow programs to "bubble
up," with the Board of Education offering encouragement
and leadership for the emergence of more locally
developed schemes. In theory, this was meant to lay the
groundwork for school constituencies and for community
school districts to develop their own programs. It was also
a recognition that change from above was not workable.

And yet, the irony of those years lay beyond these
alternatives. For, beyond those whose demands for change
were prompted by the feeling that the system was not doing
enough, were the larger number of ethnics—white and
black—for whom public educational policy really meant
jobs, social mobility, increased stability.

But if the obstacles to change in the schools were great
and if change from the top was difficult, and if Chancellor
Scribner was better in front of the cameras than in front of
a desk or an organization, the obstacles to educational
change were still more basic.

On the one hand, the demands for change reflected the
fact that certain groups felt that the school system was not
doing enough. On the other hand, demands by ethnic groups
could not really satisfy those who sought more jobs, better
living conditions, and more social mobility.

In the end, Scribner's experience showed that trying to resolve group conflict by appeal to common strains of educational reform was a tenuous strategy. A more forceful administrator might have been able to unite the diverse ethnic groups competing in school politics. More probably, though, the dominance of ethnic conflict made educational reform an unlikely strategy for satisfying these basic conflicts.

Struggling for Student Rights

As educators sought to alter the institutions of education, particularly at the secondary level, with the creation of alternative schools, students themselves were also active. Responding in part to the civil rights and antiwar movements, black, Hispanic, and white students throughout the country demanded rights: to be given hearings prior to disciplinary suspensions, to wear controversial buttons and clothing, to decide what should be published in their school newspapers.

Student rights controversies, which rocked the education establishment, began in the large cities: New York, Chicago, Philadelphia, but moved to smaller cities like Portland, Oregon, and upper-class suburbs like Great Neck, New York. Whatever their origin, the disputes over due process and free speech inevitably raised questions of ethnic dimensions. Were poor blacks and Hispanics being unfairly

suspended? Were the middle-class white students entitled
to free expression in their high school newspapers? To
what extent did free speech exacerbate the difficulties of
racial and ethnic conflict that the schools should be seeking
to reduce?

These are the issues which pervaded student rights and
transformed them from a simple assertion of civil-libertarian
sentiment into a more general expression of the basic
social conflicts affecting the schools. These conflicts
reflected the differences between the rich and the poor,
the old and the young, the black and the white.

These conflicts, which still fester, were highlighted in
New York City, the first major city to introduce a formal
statement on student rights and responsibilities.

The large public hall of the New York City Board of
Education on that mild, early September day in 1970 was
filled to capacity. The members had invited all high school
principals to comment on student rights. The press was
excluded, but Bernard Bard of the *New York Post* and
Robert Potts of CBS television prowled the hall outside.
Sprinkled throughout the hall were a few special assistants
to the Board. No one else was permitted in. The specific
subject had been decided: a discussion of the Board's
liberalization of suspension procedures designed to
guarantee due process to children and their parents. There
was more, really. The student rights code was an easy prey.

The hall was now quiet, but the impending clash of power
and status and muscle was in the air. Who, after all, had
the power? The political Board of Education: ephemeral,
too eager to compromise with organized protest, harassed,
often preoccupied? The new chancellor, who sat quietly on
the platform and carried with him the hopes for reform? Or
did it reside with the high school principals—ninety-one men
and two women (including two blacks)—who sat in the

audience, products of a system that promoted people on the basis of a grueling, often inexplicable examination that often drove the most capable and ambitious away. Or, had the day of reckoning really arrived, and was the school system on the threshold of a different—if not better—day when its constituents, students and parents and others, might demand an equal voice in governing schools?

The members relaxed, if only for the moment. It was a warm day, early in the school year, and tempers were not yet frayed, and all the old saws still sounded a bit fresh.

"You," said one principal to a Board member, "you and your lackeys refuse to answer my calls, to write me, to acknowledge me. Instead, you throw in my face the worst document ever misconceived by any school board member —students' rights."

Somebody whistled, long and low. It was a frontal attack. "Beautiful," said one listener, "beautiful."

"Incompetent," was another charge directed at a member in a steely, well-articulated voice. A man in his sixties, he was still the dean of principals, the generally accepted leader of the "hawks," a lapsed leftist who now ran an efficient school with a fist of steel. He was accustomed to respect—if not genuflection—and he expected and received that deference from his peers more for his quick mind than for his authoritarianism.

But not from Murry Bergtraum. "Don't you dare to speak to me in that way," he spat out. He was hard-faced now and upset, his eyes glistening with tears. "You act just as you say the militants do." And he leaned forward and glared down at the man at the microphone. A glass of water on his desk tipped over and fell onto the floor. The noise was audible throughout the hall. "Damn it," he said, and he stared at the speaker. "When you talk personally about us, you're beneath contempt."

"And so are you," another principal shouted back from his seat.

"I consider all this Board does garbage. I throw all your garbage messages away. If that's insubordination, make the most of it."

On the platform, no one said anything. A member scribbled on a yellow pad. A special assistant looked back at the audience. A quick head count. About twenty or thirty clapped. The others remained silent.

The principal went on. "You want to work with us, fine. If not, we'll go our own way." He then began a direct attack on a member, holding him accountable for his miseries.

The pale administrative head of the high school division sat in the rear of the room. "You *see* what I have to put up with?" he asked, his face fatigued, his body sagging.

An aide moved up to a group of younger principals. "Do those men really speak for *you?*" "No," said one of them, "not at all." "So why didn't you speak up?" Shrugs.

The Board itself had doubts about student rights and liberalized suspension procedures. Still, subjected to so emotional and blistering an attack, the members were drawn even closer together. A reasoned, more subtle case would surely have aroused their interest and even sympathy. But the attackers were for the moment beyond reason.

One year before the secretary of the Board had sent a memo to all members, detailing prior Board activities in student rights. For one thing, the previous Board had set up a committee whose major task was "to develop a code on student rights and responsibilities." The committee had met several times and reported in May 1969:

It is apparent that there are many areas of student conflict in which legitimate questions can be raised as to whether the present policies of the Board infringe on the

rights of students. Moreover, the failure to adequately
define student rights inevitably results in a failure to
define the proper scope of student responsibilities.

New York City's schools, like all others in the country, had
no coherent policy on the subject. Pupils were harassed
and often suspended from classes merely for wearing the
wrong kind of clothing or the wrong length of hair or for
distributing literature on the street. On occasion, some were
suspended from classes for being too outspoken for some
principals. After the confrontation at Ocean Hill and during
the final months of the tenure of the previous Board of
Education a student "spring offensive" began and, for the
first time in decades, some students actually revolted—and
many of them destroyed school property. Everyone was
caught unprepared. Fires, disruptions, and demonstrations
for a wide variety of causes were reported throughout the
city.

(In California, a plan was developed "to cope with
student unrest and disturbance." It recommended such
courses of action for principals as "arranging to have
movie and still pictures taken," monitoring phone calls,
calling for the police, and withholding all information from
the press.)

In New York City, on one day, Tuesday, April 22, 1969,
police reported fifty school-related incidents, with twelve
arrests. "During the last four days," wrote a member of
Mayor Lindsay's school task force, "my office has seen the
greatest number of citizen complaints that we have taken
during the past eight months. Parents all over the city were
afraid to send their children to school and in many cases
have gotten hysterical over the telephone."

Principals echoed this, telling Nathan Brown, then
Superintendent Bernard Donovan's deputy, that the
attacks were part of a centralized, coordinated plot. What

was needed, they argued, was city-wide coordination to contain them. Brown told them, "The FBI, the police and other investigative agencies are working on this matter."

There was another, even more dangerous threat. Board officials tended to confuse the problems of black and white students. A good many of the acts of disruption were carried out by some black and Puerto Rican students. They were often only a vanguard, but frequently their leaders were among the most sophisticated in the schools. They had just issued their "15 Demands," a series of categorical, "non-negotiable" demands.

Among other things, they called for the banning of police from the schools and the outlawing of all suspensions. They wanted an end to general and commercial diplomas. They sought open admission into the city's public colleges, jobs and housing for all students, the barring of the schools to military recruiters, curricular emphasis on black and Hispanic ethnic history and culture, Swahili offered in every high school, and a "decision-making student-faculty board in every high school." "Power," they screamed at public meetings, "we want student power."

It was but the beginning. The high school principals were confused and sullen. And the critics—those who had children in the public schools and, most especially, the legions who did not—were as impotent and vague as the members and the professionals. Everyone had a notion of where they were now; few knew where they wanted to go and how to get there.

Superintendent Donovan and his deputies floundered. A lifetime of paternalism and central direction was under assault from a hundred moving, guerrilla-like positions. Donovan, ever the politician, had prepared a candid, private response to the "15 Demands." But as the 1968–1969 school year drew to a close and the spring offensive abated, his answer was withheld. No one had ever before addressed themselves to black students. "Say nothing," advised a staff member, "and it'll all go away." He was right. The following school year came and went, and no more mention was ever made again by any student group of "15 Demands."

On his first day in office, Seymour Lachman received a call from the chairman of a local school board. Would he pay a personal visit to Brooklyn Technical High School? "Tech," which then housed almost 8,000 students, was one of the city's most prized possessions: a school for bright young men. Entrance was traditionally and rigorously guarded; the admission exams were difficult and arduous; those who entered the school were justifiably proud. But blacks and Puerto Ricans had recently raised a clamor. The exams, they said, were an inaccurate barometer of their potential and had turned the school into a privileged sanctuary for whites. Immediately some of the bars were dropped, with many school administrators either unable or unwilling to defend what they had for decades practiced and accepted as reasonable.

Tech, on the day when Lachman drove toward the school, had a small, but growing number of nonwhite students. His car took him past the decaying buildings of downtown Brooklyn, past treeless avenues and dirty streets, past Fort Greene Park, with its commanding monument to General Nathanael Greene of the Revolutionary War, where few people now dared walk after dusk. He mused over the dilemma: blacks demanding entry and then making demands that otherwise sensible and well-meaning people found difficult, if not impossible, to grant at this, their first-time-round with adolescents—let alone black adolescents—making "non-negotiable" demands.

Student rights. Responsibilities. Should he move ahead on this? Or should he follow the lead of other school districts and promote even more restrictions? And how to distinguish between political expressions and criminal acts? Were there limits to anyone's behavior, in or out of power?

That day, sixty blacks had been suspended at the school. They had posted a picture of Eldridge Cleaver ("All my heroes are dead, man, except Cleaver," said a student outside the building), and when an angry teacher tried to take it down, he had been stopped. They were suspended for five days; the next day other black students, four Puerto Rican students, and one white student refused to enter the school.

The school's atmosphere was electric; the principal was tense and obviously tired and at a loss as to what to do. The principal had, however, prepared a statement. If the students would agree to abide by school regulations, they could be reinstated at once. A teacher approached Lachman. Three of the kids originally suspended, he said, wanted to come back in, but many of the people in the community, who had since become involved, were pressuring them to stay out, since a larger principle was involved. They didn't want education, only confrontation, he said, moving away, shaking his head.

He was one of the two leaders of the Afro-American Students Association, speaking on a hot summer day in the office of the head of Lindsay's educational task force. "There were 'Nigger-lover' scrawls in the teachers' cafeteria, near where she sat," he said. "Mrs. Cohen was one of the few white teachers who cared about us and defended us."

The two black students were impatient and refused to go off on any tangents. "Where will you go after high school?" was met with, "Into the revolution," and "I've been suspended, I ain't going anywhere."

"The Italians and their Mafia, they shot at me twice." The

student was intense, without humor, but also uncertain. His
tuna sandwich lay scarcely touched, his Coke as yet
untasted. The only clue to his anxiety and to his anger was
his chain smoking.

It was 6:15 P.M., late session was over, and we were
leaving the school. Canarsie High was pretty new and we
were the first number of black kids of any size who were
going there. One of our girls was suddenly knifed. So we
fought. For one hour and 45 minutes we fought. And no
police ever showed up. So we called the police. Now
blacks don't usually call the police, but they still took
their time. Picture that scene. Italian parents outside
the schools with guns; blacks and Puerto Ricans inside
the building. And the principal, he was inside his office,
barricaded, locked up, afraid.

The students complained they were "not treated like
human beings." They were, they said, suspended
arbitrarily and transferred because of the color of their
skin. There was as well the question of drugs. "In my
school the Italians pushed pills and the blacks reefers and
dope, and both fought to sell to the Jews. When the whites
crossed lines, the trouble started. But they always hated us
anyway."
Their goals were vague and confused. What they wanted
were the "15 Demands" and attitudinal changes among
whites. "Nothing less," warned one before he left. "Nothing
less or the shit'll hit the fan."

Afterward, four black politicians visited the Board of
Education. They were pleasant and cheerful but almost as
aggrieved as the two students and the principals. The
Board of Education and the powers in the city had always

ignored them, they complained. "No one," said one, "has ever invited us to consult with us as equals." State Senator Waldaba Stewart, who spoke last, was the most vociferous. He had been instrumental in putting together the decentralization law in Albany. He swung his arm out and knocked over a cup of coffee. Some of the others smiled, but not Stewart. He was turning the meeting around now, moving on to the offensive, with the soft West Indian lilt still in his voice.

Student rights? We've got no answers or political advice at this time. Let the Board first treat us equally. We either have to use the back door or they ask us to rescue them after they have unilaterally decided on policy. When the teachers' strike was on, I made no public statements. When I was approached to condemn anti-Semitism, I would not answer. I condemn anti-Semitism as much as I condemn hatred against my own people, but this is important, and you have to get it through to guys more powerful than you: We want to be part of committees recommending decisions.

To be treated equally. To be treated with the deference usually reserved for the white politicians. The black politicians would help support a code, but it would have to be a collaborative project.

Later in July, a nine-page draft was presented to the Board for comment. "These are not ordinary times," it began, and it set down some preliminary thoughts. That document would soon vanish and be replaced by a shorter version and then be rewritten dozens of times more. But still the basic premise never was lost sight of: There was a large "middle ground" in the city, neither revolutionary nor obscurantist; it ranged from left to right; its members were

interested in change without panic, but, above all, change
that would protect them and their children. Personally
committed to civil liberties as well as reconciliation
between the city's warring factions, the members were
determined to make an effort, however modest, to deal with
the ferment. This meant not only to "cool" things, but to deal
as genuinely as possible with the development of long-range
guidelines that would permit peaceful protest, nonviolent
dissent, and reform within the system. Change would also
have to recognize the legitimate and leading roles of
principals and classroom teachers.

The Board's black member, Isaiah Robinson, sent his
reply: Okay as far as it goes but it doesn't go far enough.
His concern was more often with decentralization and
community control than with student rights. He was also
deeply sensitive to charges that he was less than vigorous
in defending black rights. Accused of being an "Uncle Tom"
by some black students at a public hearing, he smiled
broadly and defensively and spent much of the after-hours
with those students. He had, after all, been deeply involved
in the civil rights and community control movements while
these students were still in swaddling clothes. The next day
he took to wearing a green and black liberation button in
his lapel.

The conservative Mary Meade grumbled at private
meetings about incorrigible rowdies and the declining sense
of responsibility among the young. She would, in the end,
vote to support the document, but it was never quite clear
just why. Perhaps she sensed that the code in its final draft
represented a compromise, even if her conservative white
ethnic constituents might still feel threatened. Even so,
whenever the members were attacked by outsiders they
tended to draw together, trying desperately to avoid the
internecine wars of previous Boards.

Joseph Monserrat wanted to be associated with student rights, and he informed an audience at a public meeting, in late August 1969, that "by September 8th" the Board would produce a finished document.

During his first presidency, Joseph Monserrat called two public and very stormy meetings on the subject. To Lachman he confided, in April 1970, that, of course, he wanted the code, but it was essential that they move on from there to develop a fair governance mechanism in the schools, one that permitted changes without violence.

The student code draft, now completed, was opened up for discussion. Queens member Murry Bergtraum sent a copy to his nephew, the editor of a high school newspaper. The boy took the draft seriously, informing Bergtraum that it was in effect, a good start but left much to be desired. Bergtraum passed this off: "He's still young; wait until he grows up a little."

Donovan said very little since he saw himself as a lame duck and preferred to leave it to his successor. School superintendents are, almost by definition, careful and always mindful of their oppositon; Donovan and his successor were understandably reluctant to take on added problems. Moreover, as with so many men of power and responsibility having their first encounter with rebellion from below, he had no precedents to draw upon, no examples to follow. Distribution of student literature within school buildings and even draft counseling became established policy by September 1970, the latter with virtually no opposition. School systems across the nation, from Philadelphia to Portland, Oregon, followed New York's policy. But even more ironically, the National Educational Association and the American Federation of Teachers, by late 1970, were also calling for similar codes throughout the nation, including distribution of student proclamations

on school grounds and even the right to petition against
public agencies, governing boards, and school
administrations.

"Students," Shanker said, "should have the same rights
as those granted to teachers." He even suggested that one
day students would be engaged in collective bargaining
with school boards. In private sessions with students at
John Bowne and Julia Richmond high schools, he wowed
the kids. "I didn't realize he was so radical," said one girl
who had heard him speak on the topic. Some thought it was
a case of placating the last man out the door, a sort of
Southern-Northern strategy. But others scoffed at this. He
was a liberal, albeit not of the knee-jerk variety. He did
have mildly socialist roots, of a nondoctrinaire kind, and he
was far more willing to share in the processes of change
than his rank and file. In some instances even he had to
outflank his conservative hard-liners. At a public Board
hearing, one of his vice-presidents questioned the logic of a
student rights code without an equal stress on
responsibilities and only grudgingly offered to support it on
a "watchful waiting" basis. On the way out, another United
Federation of Teachers vice-president muttered: "You guys
have opened the floodgates. It's the beginning of the end of
high schools. I don't know how you can sleep."

A group of white women came in from Far Rockaway. They
were worried. It was raining hard that day and it had added
to their discomfort. "Why do you want to spoil our school?"
one of them, a frail and gentle women asked quietly. "It's a
good school. We voted to support our principal after he
explained to us what you were doing."

White faces, black faces, brown faces. Jewish, Irish,
Italian, and Chinese. No group was more consulted than
high school principals. But the leadership of their group
wanted the right of veto. A list of every student

government president in the city was culled, and every eighteenth, in alphabetical order, was invited in for comments. The vocational students, often the children of hyphenated Americans, were content with their roles. "We've got everything we need. We don't want the trouble you guys got," one vocational student said, pointing to the others. He was black, and his white partner shook his head in agreement. There was something about the city's vocational schools. Some said they were quiet because trouble-makers were threatened with loss of job recommendations after graduation. But others pointed with pride at the schools' records: no disorders, integrated student bodies, on-the-job training. The head of Young Americans for Freedom in a Queens high school echoed many of the complaints of his peers, but, unlike others, thought the projected code "just right." And from one high school, traditionally "middle American," with a blend of Irish, Italian, and German youngsters, came their own version of a code calling for much more: a student government independent of the administration, optional flag salutes, the right to invite speakers of their choice to the school, and "students and parents shall have the right to file complaints against school officials before a joint committee of students, teachers, and principal."

Acting Superintendent Nathan Brown was still anxious. If we have trouble, he warned the members, it will come for one of two reasons: "The principal and/or faculty is not listening to their pupils or, and I believe this may be true in most cases, some outside group will stimulate disorder." Elsewhere he said that a student code was more appropriate to college than high school, but that we had to "protect the legitimate rights of pupils," we had to "listen to and respect them." It was a tortuous path for him and he could not make up his mind. Typically, nothing might have

happened—ordinarily the code would have been studied
to death.

Donald Reeves, a black student from Music and Art High
School, quick, very bright, and deeply affected by the role
he saw himself occupying, became the public spokesman
for the High School Student Rights Coalition, actually a
handful of Students Rights Mobilization members,
overwhelmingly white. Most members of this group were
articulate, amiable in private conversation, and fervent in
their wish to inject their version of students rights into the
picture, namely, that an elected school-wide committee, in
which students dominated, would manage the high schools.
They claimed they represented 275,000 students and yet,
when challenged in one of several private sessions to prove
that by coming out for representative elections, they drew
back. They wanted, instead, approval by the Board of their
named spokespersons for all high school students and
their code being accepted as law. Their influence was very
slight, but the president of the United Parents Associations
and the executive director of the New York Civil Liberties
Union asked that they be given a hearing.

The nagging question was who represented whom? The
answer more likely was that like the adults, no one other
than the teacher and supervisor unions had any real staying
power or consistent interests. No one spoke for anyone but
him- or herself.

Even so, in February 1970, the adoption of the code
seemed doubtful. The first public meeting to discuss its
acceptance had been a shambles. Black students from the
Afro-American Students Association had taken over the
microphone and refused to yield. Robinson was singled
out for abuse. "You don't represent anyone," shouted a girl
who said she was a student. "You're only neutral."

The second meeting, which would be the last one, was

equally chaotic. Drifting in at the start were the police, the press, and television camera crews, as well as a large number of people there to make statements. A WINS reporter tried to interview some black students, and, while one of them tried to answer carefully, another grabbed the microphone, and to the screams and laughter of the others, read aloud their own "15 Demands." "Animals," said a woman, in fury.

Murry Bergtraum presided. One speaker said the wearing of buttons and armbands in schools and fewer controls over the student press could lead to extremes of behavior. A paper plane flew by his head. He waved at it, his face livid with anger. "This is the most disgraceful meeting the Board has ever held."

"Barbarians," a woman whispered. "Jungle bunnies."

"Lady, you suck," sneered one girl.

"Cannibals," she stiffened, got up, and walked up the aisle, stopping only to speak to a cop. He listened and then shrugged his shoulders.

Abe Levine, the perennial teachers union spokesman at public meetings, was on his feet, assailing a clause that would allow students to recommend their own faculty advisors for official publications. "Popularity," he began, "must not be permitted to serve as a substitute for professional competence."

Bong-Bong-Bong!

Down the aisle came another black student, this time with a battery-operated bell. Airplanes continued to fly by. Bergtraum blanched.

"There will be no flying of zeppelins here, none at all," he ordered. "Who's flying these zeppelins?" he again demanded in exasperation. Another plane went by his right ear.

"Grandpa," a boy shouted aloud, "what's a zeppelin?"

Bong-Bong-Bong!

"Order, order." "Sit down." "Shut up." "You shut up."
Members of Students Rights Mobilization huddled in a
corner. They had earlier passed out leaflets urging the
blacks to cool it, to let everybody get their turn. "That
Reeves," said one black, leaning back in his seat, "he's a
real cool brother. Together, you know? But a Tom.
Anyway you look at it, he's a Tom."

"Was there prior consultation with different groups?" a
speaker asked. There was, and for months, but no one
heard his answer.

Bong-Bong-Bong!

A black student had once again taken the microphone.
Your code's concerns are only partially ours, he was saying.
The First Amendment, which gets you all excited, takes a
back seat to illegal suspensions, cops pushing us around,
dope-pushing in schools, only winked at by the schools,
general diplomas which kill our people, and state regent
exams, which are racist.

"You people got to learn to respect us"—good enough,
honest, and, in a way, pleading—but then the extravagance
and infantilism. "Else you gonna die." Hundreds stood and
cheered, holding up their clenched fists. "Power to the
People! The People! The People!"

Several black students suddenly raced toward the
rostrum, one grabbing Robinson's name tag and another,
Meade's. She sat straight-backed, hushed, as if
Armageddon had arrived. But Meade, who had voted for the
student rights code in private session, never paled. If the
Anti-Christs had come for her, surely then she would be
ready.

Bong-Bong-Bo———!

It went hurtling over the audience and onto the stage, and
a Board aide, who would later become the youngest
college president in the country, went down, bleeding and

semiconscious. He had been struck by a flashlight battery, and it lay not two feet from him.

The student unrest so much in evidence at this meeting was not, of course, limited to New York City's schools. In Los Angeles, in 1968, five predominantly Mexican-American schools went on strike, as did predominantly black Jefferson High School, where fires were set and windows smashed. In Venice, California, eight hundred white students and nonstudents fought the police. "Two hundred young persons broke up a meeting of the City Board of Education," reported the *Los Angeles Times,* "and sent most board members fleeing out of a rear door Thursday, as a climax to a day of boycotts, arson, and the stoning of police cars at schools attended by minority groups." Other disruptions —more often than not nonviolent sit-ins—took place in Greenville, Mississippi, Teaneck, New Jersey, Miami, Florida, and in many other school districts across the national.

If it was difficult for many in authority to accept so modest, so limited, and so moderate a document as the student codes it was also hard for many of the young and their adult sympathizers to grasp the important aspect of responsibility and self-discipline built into that code.

In time, other events would push this battle into the background. School politics works this way. Moods change, passions abate, new causes and fashions receive attention, privatism enters, and some of the participants leave the public scene. But still, the code had become the law and had, in turn, established a national model.

The code was finally approved and put into effect. In retrospect, the codification of student rights neither worked so well as its proponents hoped it might, nor so poorly as its opponents predicted it would. But some immediate consequences were quickly evident. A high school principal

in Brooklyn—a vociferous, even passionate antagonist—
once spoke of his school's student newspaper: "In effect,
I'm the publisher. And how many publishers allow their staffs
complete freedom of the press?"

This sentiment was echoed nationally. One student editor
wrote to Sam Feldman, Assistant Professor of Journalism at
San Fernando Valley State College, in 1969, "Many of the
students are extremely interested in politics. Every article on
policies [ranging from reports on presidential candidates'
speeches to an attack on George Wallace] have been
stopped on the principal's desk. Again, 'Sorry, censored.' "

The same school principal who viewed himself as the
publisher of the school newspaper also wondered, "Why
should I permit girls to wear long skirts? For their own
protection—they could trip on stairways—I forbade that."
But, then, why hadn't he allowed them to wear slacks
during the frigid winter? Wasn't that for their protection?
"That's not the same thing," he argued. "Once you allow
them to choose their own school clothing you open the
door to anything. Would you let them wear see-through
blouses too?" But the code, and perhaps more signficantly,
the ferment of those years, prevented that sort of
irresponsible censorship for years afterward. The student
press now had far more freedom to discuss and, if need be,
to exhort their peers on issues that directly concerned them.
Once-forbidden pieces on the Vietnam War, the draft,
conscientious objection, and the Canadian exile, the rights
of women, and especially on race and ethnic concerns
began, slowly, to appear.

Nevertheless, the code was not basically innovative. It
merely systematized rights that court rulings and previous
Board decisions had articulated, but which had more often
than not been ignored.

Just as the demands that led to New York City's
"Statement of Student Rights and Responsibilities" began

to subside, the document which they had spawned became a model. Other school systems throughout the country from Portland, Oregon, to Philadelphia, Pennsylvania, looked to the New York experience as a guide. The New York City experience not only signaled the coming conflict, but provided a system of guidelines for its resolution.

Nationally, the late 1960s and early 1970s witnessed a rush toward student activism on college campuses and, soon after, in many high schools. Counterreactions followed among surprised and chagrined school administrators and political authorities. Left to themselves, it is doubtful that school administrations would have developed student codes of "rights" and "responsibilities." But the larger political events of those stormy years spurred protest and led to judicial intervention. The Supreme Court's decision in *Tinker* v. *Des Moines Independent Community School District,* a case brought by three Iowa public school students who had worn black armbands in school as a demonstration against the war in Vietnam, tripped off a liberal court's majority warning to school officials everywhere that student rights did not stop "at the schoolhouse gate." The *Tinker* decision's importance was its willingness to examine the legality of traditional codes of behavior set down by school districts and to judge those regulations in the light of the Constitution.

The concept of constitutional rights in the schoolhouse embraced, among others, the obligatory classroom flag salute. In states like New York, Florida, and Maryland, this requirement was challenged by protesting students. In New York City, student plaintiffs remained seated during the mandatory ceremony. School administrators, retreating before the customary practice of punishing pupils for such "misbehavior," temporized instead. They compelled the students to leave their classroom during the pledge to the flag as a condition for not joining in. The students refused,

and their suit countered—and three state courts agreed—
that such exclusion was tantamount to punishment, merely
because they had fallen back on their legal rights. The
courts ruled that school officials could not violate those
rights if the form of expression did not violate the rights of
other pupils or cause a commotion in the classroom.

In spite of *Tinker* and related decisions, some lower
courts have not wholeheartedly applied the Constitution to
student behavior. Recent instances involving suspended
students and their constitutional rights in Columbus, Ohio,
and Mena, Arkansas, however, have pointed consistently
to the fact that "students facing temporary suspensions
[i.e., up to ten days] have interests qualifying for protection
of the Due Process Clause of the Fourteenth Amendment to
the United States Constitution," or so argued the Supreme
Court in 1975 in the Columbus case.

The *Mena* case arose when several female students were
suspended for spiking soda pop with beer at a school
dance. The suspended girls and their families argued
successfully that they had been denied the due process
accorded all citizens. Indeed, the Court's ruling was so
momentous that the *American School Board Journal*
declared it would change "drastically the lives of every
school board member in the United States." The reason?
The ruling held that school board members were not entirely
immune from liability. In the specific context of disciplinary
codes within their schools, they could be held accountable
for damages under the Civil Rights Act if they knew, or
reasonably should have known, that punishments accorded
students might violate their constitutional rights. Ignorance,
concluded the *Journal,* was no excuse. This expulsion
violated the rights of the students, an act which can be "no
more justified by ignorance or disregard of settled,

indisputable law than by the presence of actual
malice. . . . [Board members must know the] basic
unquestioned constitutional rights of their students," ruled
the Court.

Court intervention aside, the tide of protest was fueled
not only by the Vietnam War, but by the coming of age of
the civil rights movement. And soon after, there came the
rise of the white ethnics. As the war ground to its disastrous
end, and as recession and joblessness spread—their chief
victims were nonwhites and the children and grandchildren
of Southern and Eastern European immigrants—the strains
among the competing groups began to show.

With this as a backdrop, then, the rise in high school
unrest has been explained in a variety of ways. Many school
authorities and parents saw in the unrest the hand of
leftwing radicalism facilely manipulating students. It was a
conspiratorial view of events, as myopic as it was
inaccurate. Other, more elaborate studies sought the reason
for the national activism. A 1970 attitudinal survey of seven
thousand students offered as a source the faulty governance
of schools. The study, sponsored by the Center for Research
and Education in American Liberties at Teachers College of
Columbia University, drew upon suburban and urban
schools in Greater New York and Philadelphia. Reflecting
their times, the respondents emphasized their desire for
just school regulations and respect for individual rights.
The Center's director, Alan F. Westin, wrote: "The great
majority of the students are angry, frustrated, increasingly
alienated by school. They do not believe they receive
individual justice or enjoy the rights of dissent or share in
critical decision-making affecting their lives within the
school." The project director, John F. DeCecco, Professor
of Psychology and Education at San Francisco State
University, added: "The absence of fair school governance"

was the key. But was it? We do not yet know with certainty, but for many protesters, it was surely a motivating factor, perhaps the greatest among many.

For a great number of the brightest and most aware students, particularly those associated with student newspapers, free speech and a free press were critical. In Houston, in 1969, an underground newspaper was banned, under a school principal's authority to "make such rules and regulations that may be necessary in the administration of the school and in promoting its best interests. He may enforce obedience to any reasonable and lawful command." The Supreme Court struck that down, ruling that students are entitled to "a rule which is drawn so as to reasonably inform the student what specific conduct is prescribed." One example of these essentially civil libertarian concerns may be found in the South Dakota guide to student rights and responsibilities that avoids the usual thou-shalt-not approach customary in school publications and substitutes instead concrete guarantees involving freedom of expression, including grooming and dress styles, and freedom from corporal punishment and police intrusion on school grounds. These rights are balanced off by citing "responsibilities," too, but always in the context of constitutional rights.

The nonwhite outbursts, mainly black in origin but often Mexican-American as well, were angrier, far more estranged from public school regulations, and more physically threatening at times. Blacks' insistence on changes was somewhat similar to that of their white peers, especially their call for the rights of privacy and reforms in governing schools. Their interest in free speech and freedom of the press was usually less and their emphasis on curtailing school suspensions usually greater. Underlying their threats and demands lay the facts of their race and heritage and the roles they had been forced to play for too many years.

Even a cursory review of their literature reveals common threads and bitterness. The *Chicano Student News* in Los Angeles in 1968 demanded that faculties be fluent in Spanish. "HOW CAN THEY EXPECT TO TEACH US IF THEY DO NOT KNOW US?" asked one editorial headline. Chicano demands included textbooks reporting Mexican and Mexican-American contributions to the United States.

Elsewhere, in Philadelphia, Baltimore, New York City, and Berkeley, among many other places, black students demanded—in New York City they used the term, "non-negotiable demands"—such purely black agenda items as the introduction of Afro-American courses and the teaching of Swahili and an end to "suspensions or expulsions of a political or asinine nature." The charge that blacks were disproportionately suspended from school was made by the United States Department of Health, Education and Welfare's Office for Civil Rights, in 1972, against the Dallas schools and, in 1976–1977, against New York City schools—and challenged by each school district.

In the autumn of 1968 and into 1969, Chicago underwent its time of racial troubles. Initially, black students of Harrison High School, once mainly Czech and then 55 percent black, struck with a lengthy list of grievances. They wanted a black principal, more black teachers, a black ROTC commander, in short, black control of Harrison. They wanted, they said, *their* food in the cafeteria, better vocational education, and "more homework." Not all black pupils agreed, and two hundred of them signed a petition that good teachers, and not necessarily black ones, were important to them.

Throughout Chicago, other schools erupted. At Austin High School in the western part of the city, demonstrations began. Lily-white five years earlier, it was 49 percent black in 1968. When black activists presented demands similar to those made at Harrison, two hundred white students boycotted the school, which, in turn, led to black sympathy strikes at three other high schools the following day.

On October 15, twenty-eight thousand students, mostly black, stayed away from thirty-two Chicago high schools. One hundred and twenty-five Spanish-speaking students picketed Lake View High School on the North Side for help in English, plus courses related to their ethnic backgrounds. These racially motivated disturbances continued into 1969, as the Board of Education strove to dash cold water on the revolt by appointing a large number of black administrators. This maneuver only caused the resentment of white ethnics to spill over, already upset as they were by the larger civil rights movement and the tendency, as many of them saw it, to extract all sacrifices in behalf of blacks from them. Parents in the far southwestern section of the city threatened a mass demonstration if black youngsters were ever sent to "their" neighborhood elementary schools.

In New York's schools, "Nigger Go Home" buttons began to appear. "They" were getting "everything," charged bitter white students. The real "enemies" were far away: opponents of continued federal spending, an eroding tax base, an unstable economic system, the fleeing white and black middle classes. What resulted was that nonwhites and ethnics, with many common denominators binding them together, now began to play out their hoary roles as competitors at the lower ends of the economic spectrum.

The outcome was that the cause of the essentially white student rights movement would continue to be furthered even after the end of campus turmoil. Federal courts would also continue, if less dramatically than before, to attempt to maintain the rights already achieved. In one such instance, Manhattan Federal Court Judge Constance Baker Motley ordered Stuyvesant High School officials to permit the distribution of a sex questionnaire to eleventh- and twelfth-grade students on First Amendment grounds. "This type of independent investigation"—wrote the judge—"should be encouraged and applauded, for an integral role of the educational system is to stimulate inquiry as well as to impart knowledge."

But, again, there will be setbacks. Judge Motley's ruling was essentially reversed in 1977 (*Trachtmen* v. *Anker*). The appellate court backed the complaining school officials when they declared that "distribution of [the] sex questionnaire would result in significant emotional harm to number[s] of students throughout the school population." And in April 1977, the conservative majority in the Supreme Court voted 5–4 that students have no constitutional protection against spanking or other forms of corporal punishment. The Court's majority opinion was written by Lewis F. Powell, Jr., in a case involving two Miami, Florida, junior high school boys. The central issue was not the students' claims of excessive and incapacitating punishment, but whether schoolchildren, like prisoners, are protected by the Eighth Amendment of the Bill of Rights, which prohibits "cruel and unusual punishments," and by "due process" before punishment. The Court majority argued that teachers may use "reasonable but not excessive" physical punishment; if that force is "unreasonable" or "excessive," it continued, school authorities can be prosecuted through civil or criminal suits. But, more significantly, the Court decided that schoolchildren have no constitutional right to any hearings whatsoever before the paddling is inflicted or on whether the punishment is justified.

Historically, the use of physical means to punish students has been common, although today two states and New York City ban corporal punishment entirely. Elsewhere, it is only occasionally utilized, although twenty-one states specifically allow its use. Still, it would appear to be a

specious reading, indeed, and incomplete justice to exclude
schoolchildren from constitutional protection. It is a judicial
judgment that will not go unchallenged.

Although student rights reflected the conflict between
young and old, it also had ethnic roots. Young black
students brought up in an era of ethnic assertiveness sought
their own self-expression in high school rebellion. Joining
forces with white student activists trained in the civil rights
and antiwar movements, they succeeded in building a strong
movement for recognition.

Integration, Busing, and Community Control Revisited[*]

In the late 1960s, community control replaced integration as a rallying cry for the black and Hispanic poor seeking to influence educational policy in the large cities.

Integration, however, did not disappear and controversies still raged about de facto versus de jure segregation, the limits of the *Brown* case, and the effect of community control on integration.

The historic *Brown* case was the first in a series of

---

[*] The authors are indebted to Larry Lavinsky for his assistance in interpreting the legal aspects of desegregation.

decisions, statutes, and executive orders that in a single generation, profoundly altered the educational, economic, social, and political fabric of the United States. Not only have we largely exorcised dual systems of public education, but also the separate restrooms and lunch counters, the separate seating sections on trains and buses, the empty voting rolls, and the blatant job discrimination that characterized the racism under which blacks had for so long labored.

If the *Brown* decision set the stage for this great transformation, the Civil Rights Act of 1964, one of the outstanding achievements of Lyndon B. Johnson's Presidency, served as the main catalytic agent. Title IV of the Civil Rights Act authorized the Department of Justice to bring suit against school districts maintaining segregation. Title VI used even stronger language, authorizing the denial of funds under any federal program for a district that practiced segregation. The carrot and the stick were now firmly in the hands of federal officials.

Over two decades after *Brown,* the optimism of 1954 has been largely dissipated, with a resulting sense of frustration and confusion. Many people agree with Tom Wicker, associate editor and national columnist of the *New York Times,* that this nation no longer has a coherent policy for school integration.

Court decisions unequivocally condemning state-mandated segregation coupled with the threat of economic sanctions by the federal government were potent forces in bringing an end to the dual school systems of the South. They were far less effective in dealing with the largely de facto segregation in the North. Demographic changes and the flight of middle-class whites and blacks from the cities have relentlessly eroded school desegregation efforts. Contradictory evidence compiled by social scientists has created a controversy as to the educational and psychological effects of desegregation.

For a variety of reasons, involuntary busing has become a national issue, as seething resentment has flared into racial violence, and politicians, sensing the mood of their constituents, have supported various types of antibusing legislation.

Desegregation and the Law

In its school desegregation decisions, the Supreme Court has made a legal distinction between de jure and de facto segregation. The former involves intentional governmental action. The latter does not. Because of this distinction, civil rights forces, largely victorious in battling the many state-mandated "dual" school systems in the seventeen Southern and border states and the District of Columbia, have had far less success in attempting to desegregate the school systems of the North.

Brown held that it was impermissible under the Constitution for the states, or their instrumentalities, to force children to attend segregated schools. But the nature of the remedy was not even discussed in the initial *Brown* decision. In its second *Brown* decision, handed down in 1955, the Court placed the primary responsibility for formulating plans to effectuate "transition to a racially non-discriminatory school system" upon school authorities, subject to court review. Interestingly, the Court spoke in terms of *"non-discrimination"* rather than "desegregation."

There soon arose a question whether affirmative state action to desegregate was required or whether state neutrality, permitting freedom of choice as to schools attended, was sufficient, so long as the state assured that the choice was genuinely free of official restraint. A number of decisions in the lower courts upheld "freedom of choice" programs. However, this interpretation was rejected by the Supreme Court in *Green* v. *County School Board of New Kent County* (1968).

Green articulated the affirmative duty concept in the "elimination of racial discrimination" within a rural setting. It remained for the Court in *Swann* v. *Charlotte-Mecklenberg Board of Education* (1971) to articulate and define that duty in the sprawling urban school system of metropolitan Charlotte, North Carolina.

Charlotte-Mecklenberg is actually one of eighteen of the country's hundred largest school districts that contain both the central city and the surrounding surburban county in one school district. Therefore, even though the city of Charlotte is only 64 square miles, the United School District of Charlotte-Mecklenberg County (with one board of education) is actually 550 square miles, or almost twice the size of New York City's school district.

In what was to be the last major unanimous decision by the Court on the subject of school desegregation, Chief Justice Warren Burger authorized compulsory busing, among a variety of other methods "to eliminate from the public schools all vestiges of state-imposed segregation."

Swann was both the high point in the movement toward school desegregation and a harbinger of the many problems that would emerge in the 1970s. For, if the Court went further in that case than in any other to enunciate the many approaches available "to dismantle dual school systems," it also made it quite clear that "judicial powers may be exercised only on the basis of a constitutional violation," and that the violation to be remedied was "state-enforced separation of races in public schools."

Furthermore, the Court rejected the concept of imposing any particular degree or quota of racial balance.

Finally, in 1973, *Keyes et al.* v. *School District No. 1, Denver, Colorado, et al.* reached the United States Supreme Court, and for the first time the nation's highest tribunal dealt with a Northern school system where no statutory dual system had ever existed.

The majority of the Court adhered to the de facto/de jure distinction. However, it also held that, in view of the school board's "intentionally segregative actions in a meaningful portion of [the] school system," the board had "the burden of proving that other segregated schools within the system are not also the result of intentionally segregative actions."

In *Milliken v. Bradley* (1974) the majority of the Court voted to prevent the implementation of a metropolitan desegregation plan for Detroit. *Milliken* ended twenty years of court decisions supportive of school desegregation by rejecting a multidistrict plan that would have included the suburbs as a means of eliminating de jure segregation in the city of Detroit.

From a legal standpoint, the *Milliken* decision represents the extension of legal concepts in earlier cases to resolve a problem not previously presented to the Court. From a practical standpoint, however, it establishes a precedent that will probably make far more difficult the attainment and maintenance of schools that are not racially identifiable in most of our nation's largest urban centers. By fortifying the suburbs as sanctuaries against busing, the decision tends to encourage middle-class flight from the cities, thereby providing a further impetus to the startling changes in demography that have occurred between 1954's *Brown* decision and 1974's *Milliken* decision.

While the United States Supreme Court was making these decisions, striking demographic changes were taking place

in our nation's urban centers, complicating and compounding
the problem further.

The Demographic Problem

The great promise of the *Brown* decision has ironically been
fulfilled in the South far more than it has in the North.
Recent figures available from the Department of Health,
Education and Welfare now reveal that in the 32 Northern
and Western states, 72 percent of black students attended
schools with a black majority, while only 28 percent attended
schools that had a white majority. In the 11 states of the
old Confederacy, where ten years ago 99 percent of black
children were in schools that were overwhelmingly black
and only 1 percent in integrated, white-majority schools,
there has been a major transformation. Today 54 percent
of black pupils attend majority black schools and fully 46
percent of black pupils attend majority white schools.
Residential patterns in the South, where blacks and whites
frequently live in the same neighborhoods or on the same
streets, have helped in bringing about this great change over
the last decade. Nationally, more than 90 percent of the 2.5
million black pupils have at least some white classmates.
But the gains in the South—brought about through the
elimination of de jure segregation—are somewhat offset
by the growing de facto segregation in the Northern cities.
    Throughout the 1950s and 1960s, black families in rural
Southern communities traveled north seeking a better life
for themselves and their children in the polyglot cities
of the North. At the same time, middle-class urban residents
were leaving the central cities, seeking a better life in the
suburbs. There is no doubt that many of the middle-class
and overwhelmingly white families were leaving because
ever increasing numbers of the poor were entering the

cities, but this was a historic pattern that was repeating itself.

Over a hundred years ago, middle-class white Anglo-Saxon native American families left for the suburbs, when the poorer Irish and German immigrants came to the cities of the United States. At the turn of the century, the more affluent descendants of those Irish and German immigrants, struggling to maintain what they perceived as their middle-class self-image, moved to the suburbs when newer and poorer immigrants—this time largely Italians, Slavs, and East European Jews—arrived to settle in the cities. Recently, we have witnessed the flight of their middle-class descendants, and of some middle-class blacks as well, when the cities of the North and West became a haven of opportunity for poor blacks, Puerto Ricans, and Chicanos.

Unlike many Europeans, Americans are not overly attached to their central cities where their collective memories go back only a few generations. They are, therefore, less inclined to stay and more interested in shaping new lives for their families in the suburban rings surrounding the cities. Those middle-class white ethnics and blacks who remain in the cities have divided their loyalties between the public and private-parochial schools. A startling example of this is the fact that over 40 percent of middle-class black families send their children to private rather than public schools.

Thus has there been forged a new kind of school segregation in the North, based more on socioeconomic factors than on race. This accelerating pattern of outmigration over the last generation has affected school systems throughout the North and West, including Washington, D.C. The nation's capital, one of the five school districts named in the *Brown* decision, had a 53 percent black student population in 1951–1952. Twenty years later, in 1972, the school population was upwards of 95 percent

black, with only 5,000 white students in a school system of
140,000 children. Court-ordered "desegregation" of a
school system already 90 percent black in 1967 further
accelerated the change, bringing it up to 97 percent
minority students in 1975. But Washington, D.C., appears,
unfortunately, to be only an advanced case of a problem
that afflicts other urban areas. By 1975, Chicago's school
population was 75 percent black and Hispanic, while in 1955
it was only 30 percent; Detroit's school population was 78
percent minority in 1975 as against only 29 percent in 1955;
Philadelphia's school population was 67 percent minority
in 1975 as against 39 percent in 1955; Los Angeles' school
population was 60 percent minority in 1975 as against 24
percent in 1955. Compounding the problem are the suburbs
contiguous to these urban areas as well as to each other. For
example, Beverly Hills, California, which has a minority
student population of 6 percent lies next to Compten, which
has a minority student population of 98 percent. Similarly,
outside Detroit, Michigan, two contiguous suburban districts
reflect this disparity. The Inkester School District has a
93 percent minority student population, while the Dearborn
Heights School District has only a 2 percent minority
population. In general, however, the suburban rings
around the major urban centers are overwhelmingly white
in student population. The general suburban population
outside Los Angeles was in 1975 only 8 percent minority
as against 4 percent minority in 1955—a minuscule increase.
The overall suburban minority population surrounding the
city of Detroit actually remained the same, at a low of 4
percent between 1955 and 1975.

The difficulties that integration plans faced are evident
in one Southern city that has had to confront integration.
Atlanta is a symbol of the progressive, industrial post–Civil
Rights Act South. Its black middle class is probably more
secure and influential than that of any large city in the nation.

It is a city that likes to say it is "too busy to hate." Today, even its urbane and progressive black Mayor Maynard Jackson would admit Atlanta faces many of the same problems as New York and its sister cities of the North and West. According to an analysis for the *New York Times* (October 7, 1974), even Atlanta's confidence in its future progress has begun to falter. And one of the city's greatest problems is believed to be its schools. In 1958, when school desegregation efforts began, they were 70 percent white. Today they are almost 90 percent black.

In August 1973, the national office of the National Association for the Advancement of Colored People (NAACP) removed the chairman of its Atlanta branch, Lonnie King, Jr., along with other local NAACP officers, because of a compromise desegregation plan that they had worked out with Atlanta city officials and federal judges (including Judge Griffin Bell of the Fifth Circuit Court of Appeals—later to become United States Attorney General). The plan, supported by the overwhelming majority of the black community, including Mayor (then Vice-Mayor) Maynard Jackson, was described by King as a compromise to enable blacks to gain control of the school system while attempting to curtail further white flight from the city. The plan, which had been approved both by the Federal District Court and by the United States Court of Appeals for the Fifth Circuit, had as its principal desegregation objective an increase in black enrollment in predominantly white schools to a level of 30 percent, with a corollary commitment by the board of education to hire a black superintendent of schools and to place blacks in about 50 percent of the system's top administrative posts.

It came down to a choice of a breakthrough in securing blacks important administrative and professional positions in the school system rather than attempting massive "integration" of a system predominantly black via long-distance busing. Many of Atlanta's large black middle-class population considered such busing to be both demeaning and unnecessary.

However, the plan has gone into effect. For the first time in its history, Atlanta, Georgia, in July 1973, selected a black man, Dr. Alonzo A. Crim, as its superintendent of schools.

The issue of integration, which was dealt with on a city-wide basis in Atlanta during the 1970s, had progressed to a different stage in New York City. After the struggle of the late 1960s brought decentralization to New York City, the issue of integration was overshadowed. It eventually emerged, however, in a new and more complicated form. Now a central Board with responsibility for bringing about integration had to contend with a community board that had initial responsibility for zoning within the district.

Case Study of Canarsie

Few school issues during the early 1970s aroused as much furor and passion as did the Canarsie boycott by white parents, who were protesting the assignment by the central Board of Education of black students from Brownsville's Tilden Houses to schools in their neighborhoods. Seizing the slogan and the spirit of resistance it encouraged, parents used the argument of community control as a rationalization for their actions as they sought to bar Tilden Houses' black children from the seventh grade. Shades of Ocean Hill–Brownsville! How had all this started? What was the background to the issues involved—issues that were misinterpreted not only in the United States but also in the Soviet Union, where a leading newspaper featured the worst aspects of the dispute. And there were many negative aspects to select from.

It might all have been avoided. Visions of Little Rock in 1956. White parents screaming curses on small black children. Marches, denunciations, anguish, and threats. Three diminutive, rather inconsequential men were suddenly caught up in a drama that received world attention: Jack Zimmer, chairman of Community School Board 18 (which includes Canarsie and East Flatbush), the Reverend Wilbert Miller, representing the blacks, and Chancellor Harvey Scribner.

Some people insisted that parents follow a course of action that would lead to snarling mobs. Others, who themselves were far removed from troubled schools and neighborhoods, offered panaceas to white and black parents of limited income whose children attended public schools.

Fear ran amok. Ugly mobs. Terrible threats. Grotesque scars. And especially the impact upon the children who were used as pawns. All the children, both black and white, had been victimized by the fear of white parents that their fragile and recent economic security and their physical safety—as they perceived it—were jeopardized by the presence of 31 more blacks in "their" white schools. "They're only the beginning of a flood, you'll see," was often heard on the streets. It was arrant nonsense, but they sincerely believed it, and some of their leaders cultivated these fears to the utmost. Where, they asked, had any school that had already "tipped" survived as an effective institution of learning? Were children learning the "three R's" in any ghetto school? The parents of JHS 68 pointed with pride to their educationally proficient children, as did the parents of JHS 211. JHS 68 ranked in testing among the top ten junior high schools in the city. JHS 211, which had 30 percent black and Puerto Rican students, was thirtieth on the city list of 158 schools; JHS 285, with more than half its student population nonwhite, scored 36 in reading—which is still very high. Two other junior high schools in the district ranked 81st and 129th, respectively. Therefore, the parents insisted, "Canarsie schools for Canarsie children." Again, that was too categorical and, therefore, sheer nonsense. In the city, children were achieving in some inner-city schools, such as in neighboring Crown Heights and in Jamaica, but the parents would not hear otherwise. Then, too, Canarsie is hardly an island unto itself or even a separate neighborhood. But, seizing the slogan and the spirit of resistance it encouraged, these parents rationalized their actions and barred Tilden Houses' black children from the seventh grade.

Junior High School 285 was named the Meyer Levin School, after the bombardier assigned to Colin Kelly's plane during the Japanese attack against the Philippines in 1941. Kelly and Levin. Levin and Kelly. In those days, it was designed to signify brotherhood and fellowship. Like the four chaplains of different faiths who went down with their torpedoed ship. Togetherness. Unity.

East Flatbush, unlike the adjoining neighborhood of Canarsie, was a pre–World War II development. It had its rows of cultivated detached and semi-attached private houses, its two- and three-story walkups, its tree-lined streets and excellent municipal services, its crowded shopping centers along Church and Utica avenues—in fact, a stereotype of a middle-class area. During the late 1960s, it began changing. By 1972, its schools were three-quarters black. These blacks were newcomers from the Caribbean, from St. Vincent, Aruba, the Dominican Republic, Haiti, Guyana, Barbados, and all the other islands and countries that dot that vast southern sea. And their overt standards of behavior, the goals they held for their young, and the propriety they carried with them everywhere were not too different from those of the whites who had arrived fifty years before. If class, and not race, is the real barrier among people, if, indeed, racial harmony requires, as a columnist once wrote, "a sense of neighborhood integrity, where ethnic and racial groups make themselves safe from people who don't like them," then the Caribbeans and the whites who remained in East Flatbush were evidence of that. Together, many of them struggled against the tactics of the blockbusters and the municipal efforts to introduce low-income housing in their midst.

Meyer Levin Junior High School was the focus of their attention. It had had, traditionally, a largely Jewish student body; it was a well-managed school which had sent many of its graduates to college. When it first opened its doors in 1956, the Anti-Defamation League of B'nai B'rith had favored zoning which would insure its racial integration.

By 1967, Levin was 22.7 percent black and 10.2 percent Puerto Rican. In 1971, whites constituted 42 percent of the student population. That figure did not meet the area's definition of integration, but, for the white resident in a neighborhood still safe, that would do. But, the white parents said, in an ever-increasing crescendo, no more nonwhites. Otherwise, the remaining whites would leave, for they had seen other schools and neighborhoods "tip." The commonly accepted, if unproven, rule was that, with more than 35 percent nonwhites in any school, scholastic achievement would drop off dramatically and the consequent problems of ghetto schools quickly arise. For many of the Caribbeans, the same rule held. They could live with the present racial distribution, but further changes endangered their property values, their life's work, their children's futures. Besides, many of them knew of the too-common decline of public services after whites had fled.

Tilden Houses was planned as an integrated housing project at a time when Brownsville was still an integrated community. By the time the project opened in 1962, Brownsville had changed and was rapidly becoming overwhelmingly black. A housing project that was initially

planned to maintain integration opened up to almost
all-black families in an almost all-black neighborhood.
But that was not unusual in the City of New York, then or
now. At that time, in the early 1960s, Brownsville, East
Flatbush, and Canarsie were all one school district. Then,
in 1964, the district split, since the student population had
grown quite large, and an attempt was made to create
smaller, more manageable districts.

In 1970, district boundaries were again shuffled. Some
students entered the new District 23, which also
incorporated the schools of the Ocean Hill–Brownsville
Demonstration District. The other Brownsville children
were either in District 18 or District 17. From 1970 on, the
Tilden Houses children, depending upon which building
they lived in, attended elementary or junior high schools
in Districts 17, 18, and 23. They were primarily, however,
in District 18.

When the Tilden Houses project opened, the schools of
East Flatbush were more than 85 percent white. The Tilden
Houses students from Brownsville were consequently sent
into East Flatbush to receive a more integrated education
as well as to increase the utilization of the schools. By
September of 1972, JHS 285's ethnic balance had changed
drastically, and the parents association believed the school
had begun to tip. The school's racial balance had reached
a point where continued and accelerated change was
certain. The school was at that time 52 percent black
and 48 percent white. The five elementary schools in East
Flatbush, where the children from Tilden Houses were sent,
had completely changed in the last decade. The students
who were supposed to receive a more integrated
education in East Flatbush schools were now attending
elementary schools that were approximately 75 percent
black and 25 percent white. The East Flatbush neighborhood
was rapidly changing and black middle-class and working-

class homeowners and tenants began moving into the area. Blockbusting was rampant and its impact was naturally felt by many who believed that the schools had symbolic value for the neighborhood. The last East Flatbush junior high school that came close to integration was 285. The parents association leadership, both black and white, believed that 285 had to be stabilized or else it would become segregated, but this time segregated as a black school rather than as a white school. If JHS 285 became segregated, the people of East Flatbush felt that the outstanding academic high school, which was across the street from the junior high school, would soon tip and become segregated. That school was Samuel J. Tilden High School. It is the only high school in East Flatbush, and, rightly or wrongly, the residents of that community felt that, if that high school were to become overwhelmingly black, then the area would become all black even more rapidly and would eventually become completely segregated—and a replica of Brownsville.

But the East Flatbush residents had other problems. They were part of Community School Board 18, which had five members from Canarsie and four from East Flatbush, and those two factions were moving farther and farther apart. At the time of the 1970 community school board elections, churches and synagogues sponsored various candidates for community school boards and worked very hard to get them elected in order to enhance the possibility of federal aid to nonpublic schools. This controversy affected the close election of Jack Zimmer, as chairman of the board in 1970 because of his strong separation-of-church-and-state position.

But by 1971, within East Flatbush, concern among blacks and whites had shifted to their prize junior high school—285—which appeared to be on the verge of tipping. A series of meetings were held, in the spring of 1971, between

Community School Board 23 and its chairman, Assemblyman Samuel Wright, and Community School Board 18 and its chairman, Jack Zimmer. These meetings, pushed by the East Flatbush contingent on Zimmer's board, culminated in a written agreement that held that schoolchildren in Tilden Houses would be assigned to Districts 20, 21, and 22 (elsewhere in Brooklyn), providing that seats would be made available to them in those areas. These three districts were between 70 and 80 percent "Other" and were receiving about 6,000 open enrollment children, who made up almost half of the total open enrollment children in the entire city. Some seats were located in these districts for the 1971–1972 school year.

In the spring of 1972, the chancellor, through his deputy, decided that no further seats should be made available to the Tilden Houses for seventh-grade children in Districts 20, 21, and 22, since Districts 16 and 17 had greater problems of overutilization and had requested 2,000 additional seats in those three integrated Brooklyn districts. The office of the chancellor strongly believed, and was subsequently upheld by the Board, in its ruling that if no seats were available under optional assignment in more integrated districts, then children could not be sent to less integrated districts.

On July 5, 1973, Deputy Chancellor Irving Anker sent a memorandum to District 18 Chairman Jack Zimmer requesting compliance with the zoning regulation that those Tilden Houses children graduating from the five elementary schools in District 18 should continue to be zoned into JHS 285 "or into other middle schools of District 18." "We must inform you," wrote Anker, "that it is our intention to take the necessary steps to enforce our legal responsibilities in this matter."

On September 11, 1972, dozens of white and black

parents stood in front of the doors of JHS 285, denying entry to Tilden Houses children who were zoned into that school. Thus, the lesser known, little publicized East Flatbush boycott had begun. They demanded that these children go to schools in another district. The community school board, which had the authority to send these children into any junior high school in the district, instead chose to appeal Chancellor Scribner's decision that these Tilden Houses students remain instead in District 18 and attend junior high schools there.

On September 19, 1972, the central Board upheld the chancellor and stated that the Tilden Houses children graduating from the sixth grade in District 18 should continue with their peers to junior high schools in District 18 and could not be sent into District 23.

On the same day Zimmer directed the Tilden children to attend JHS 252, a 90 percent black junior high school in the district. He did so in a letter to Deputy Chancellor Anker. Meanwhile, the chancellor had appointed a trustee, for the purpose of insuring compliance with the instructions that the Tilden Houses children graduating from PS 135, 233, 235, 244, and 268 in the East Flatbush section of District 18 gain admittance to JHS 285 or any other school in that district. After the chancellor received notification from Zimmer that they interpreted the ruling to mean that he could send the children to overwhelmingly black JHS 253, rather than to 285 or the junior high schools in Canarsie, Anker responded with a letter to Zimmer and other community school board members on September 22, 1972. At that time, he stated categorically,

I am directing your board at the instruction of Chancellor Scribner to assign the Tilden Housing children at the junior high school level either to JHS 285, which has been the assigned school by decision of your board for these children until now, and/or to other schools in your district where integrated education would be possible.

He did this after two other parents groups in East Flatbush had appealed to the chancellor to prevent the majority of the Board from putting these children into racially imbalanced schools, while other alternatives were available in another (Canarsie) part of the district.

The lines were now drawn and were quite clear. The chancellor and deputy chancellor had demanded that the Tilden Houses children either attend JHS 285 or one of the two junior high schools in Canarsie, JHS 211, which was approximately 70 percent "Other," or JHS 68, which was 98 percent "Other." It was felt by both the chancellor and the deputy chancellor that Canarsie was not carrying out its fair share of integration and getting away with it because they dominated Community School Board 18.

When the members of the central Board of Education informally discussed the situation, they agreed that the Tilden Houses children who were denied admittance to JHS 285 should be sent to JHS 68 without any equivocation or vacillation. They believed this to be the only feasible resolution of the controversy. Members of the central Board wanted to preserve integration and stabilize East Flatbush and, at the same time, encourage integration in Canarsie schools. The Board was particularly incensed by threats of some local school board people that "blood would flow in the streets" if the children were sent to JHS 68.

Zimmer responded to the deputy chancellor's letter of September 22 by asking for more time before sending the children into JHS 68. The Board believed that the chancellor would assign the Tilden children to JHS 68. Instead, on October 11, 1972, Deputy Chancellor Irving Anker sent a memo to Jack Zimmer, the chairman of Community School

Board 18, that had been "prepared upon the instructions of Dr. Scribner" and included the following regulations:

1. The siblings of children now attending JHS 285-K are to be admitted to classes at JHS 285 if they have not already on their own initiative registered elsewhere.
2. The balance of the junior high school students residing in Tilden Houses are to be assigned to JHS 211, if they have not already on their own initiative registered elsewhere.
3. Fifty seats are to be made available at JHS 68 to increase the degree of integration at this school for pupils now zoned in JHS 285 and JHS 211 who elect to accept this transfer.
4. In three months, Community School Board 18 is to present a plan to this office for the rezoning of JHS 285 and JHS 68 so as to more nearly equalize integration in these schools starting with the 1973–1974 school year.

On October 17, the first sit-in and boycott occurred in Canarsie at JHS 211. On Friday, October 20, Jack Zimmer received a telephone call from Chancellor Scribner, after the chancellor had been advised by various political and community groups in Canarsie. The chancellor asked Zimmer, if he, the chancellor, was now to change his mind and send the Tilden Houses children from 211 to 68, would Zimmer and Community School Board 18 support this move? Zimmer answered affirmatively and in the next day or two prepared an agreement which the chancellor then signed next to Zimmer's name, officially taking the Tilden Houses children, who had been assigned the week before to JHS 211, out of 211 and placing them in JHS 68.

The central Board of Education and the majority of Community School Board 18 first learned of this "agreement" in their morning newspapers. There was an uproar. The four East Flatbush members of the community board were incensed, not only because they had not been consulted, but also by the fact that, even though the plan still reiterated some of the provisions of the October eleventh memorandum for a more equitable rezoning of the three junior high schools, it left out the important second point, which was to have opened up fifty additional seats in JHS 68 for students from JHS 285 or 211 who elected to transfer to that school. One member of the New York State Board of Regents called Dr. Scribner's action a "racist compromise."

There was an immediate appeal by the Tilden Houses parents and the four East Flatbush members. Mayor Lindsay actually placed two telephone calls to members of the Board of Education, urging them not to overrule the chancellor and warning them that the chancellor had threatened to resign if he was overruled.

Nonetheless, on October 26, the Board of Education overruled Chancellor Scribner and stated that the children should remain at JHS 211 and not be sent to JHS 68. On October 27, Community School Board 18 appealed the Board of Education's decision to State Education Commissioner Nyquist. Again—within forty-eight hours—because of the emergency situation, Commissioner Nyquist upheld the central Board of Education's overruling of the chancellor. The children were to remain at 211.

Scribner said he still disagreed with the Board's decision, but that he would personally lead the 31 students into 211, although he still maintained 68 was the better place for them. But by this time, the chancellor's vacillation was taken by the Canarsie people as a sign of weakness. A few days later, Shanker led JHS 211's union teachers past pickets into their school following harassment and threats by the boycotting whites.

On Sunday morning, five thousand people gathered in the Canarsie Theater and were urged by speaker after speaker, both lay and clerical, never to admit the 31 students. Few, in the theater or in the city, exerted any moral leadership. People accused one another of racism and worse. Still, the major issue now confronting the Board was that the central authority of the Board of Education was being challenged by a community school board.

After numerous meetings, community leaders, including the clergy and the president of the Parent Teacher Association, accepted Scribner's offer to remove his representative and return 211 to Community School Board 18, thus guaranteeing the security and entry of students. The first boycott was at an end.

But the difficulties had not come to an end. Three different hearings took place at Junior High School 211, 68, and 285 involving the rezoning of the three schools. These hearings soon brought to the surface the bitter scars, the animosities, and even the hatreds that existed between the East Flatbush and the Canarsie board members, parents association leaders, parents, and just plain citizens. At one of the hearings, fistfights began among community residents and homeowners from East Flatbush and Canarsie.

On January 8, 1973, Community School Board 18 submitted its official rezoning proposal to Chancellor Scribner. In essence, the plan submitted by Community School Board 18 would contain the following percentage of "Other" by 1975: JHS 285, 50 percent; JHS 68, 85 percent; JHS 211, 70 percent. It would also start phasing out Tilden Houses children in the second year of the plan and complete it in the third year. At that time, no Tilden Houses sixth-graders graduating from elementary school would be accepted in District 18 junior high schools. On January 31, 1973, Scribner accepted in part the zoning proposals of District 18 and modified them by not including a third year and omitting the start of the phasing out in the second year, but leaving the door partially ajar by stating that there would be a review of the situation. After considering not hearing the appeal while the boycott continued, the Board decided to proceed.

On March 30, 1973, the Board of Education reached its decision. Many people were surprised to discover that it was a unanimous decision. The appeal decision stated that no child then attending school in District 18 would be denied the completion of his elementary and junior high school education in that district. On the other hand, since District 18 was then 52 percent "Other" and 48 percent "Minority," and dropping in its percentage of "Other" students by a projected 3 percent each year, it guaranteed that the then preschool and unborn Tilden Houses children would receive a superior integrated education for many years to come by being zoned into Districts 20, 21, and 22, where 70 to 80 percent of the students were listed as "Other." This would also give immediate integrative relief to the first grades of the five East Flatbush schools, which the Tilden Houses children were attending. It would also immediately give Tilden Houses children who were beginning their school education a better integrated educational experience than that which was being received by older Tilden Houses children who were and would be attending school in District 18.

Some of the more affluent Canarsie families had already begun talking of sending their children to private schools or of moving from the neighborhood if the boycott continued much longer. Zimmer, whose position had eroded, decided to grit his teeth and accept the decision. He had not realized in October what would result from organizing "community support" for his first boycott. Furthermore, the Board's decision offered him a partial face-saving cover for a strategic retreat. After some persuasion, the

Community School Board of District 18 decided to carry out limited integration in Canarsie.

As skeptical as some might have been, the Board of Education meant what it said when it stated that it wanted Canarsie to carry its fair share of integration in the district. Acting Chancellor Anker, in fact, rejected the plan submitted by the majority of Community School Board 18 on June 4 for achieving better integration in the elementary schools in the district. Again, on September 12, 1973, Anker directed that a revised plan for the greater integration of key elementary schools in District 18 be submitted to him by November 15, 1973. Yet, the Board of Education's actions were not received well by everybody. On May 11, 1973, at the Title I Elementary and Secondary Education Act (ESEA) hearings, a member of the State Board of Regents stood up and vowed to get every single member of the Board of Education removed and do everything possible until his last breath in this endeavor because of what he believed was its "racist Canarsie decision." On the other hand, Chief Judge Jacob Mishler, of the Federal District Court, in a decision of August 20, 1973, found that "The City Board of Education, in adopting its plan of March 31, 1973, was unaffected by local racial prejudice of the residents in District 18 or any other community district." New York State Commissioner of Education Ewald Nyquist ruled similarly on August 29, 1973, and upheld the Board's Canarsie decision as being legally and educationally sound and as being in the best interests of education.

In January 1977, four years after the Canarsie decision, Commissioner Ewald Nyquist, acting on the basis of new demographic and statistical information supplied to him by the New York City Board of Education, rescinded a December 1975 order calling for the integration of three junior high schools in District 18: 285, 211, and 68—the very three involved in the 1972–1973 Canarsie dispute. The

new information revealed, the commissioner said, that his
original order to integrate JHS 285 by equalizing the ethnic
percentages of students at the three schools "would
seriously threaten the continued integrated status" of
JHS 211 and 68, would hasten the flight of white families
from the area, and would thus be "counterproductive."
Nyquist asked the New York City Board of Education to
submit a plan that would "provide other ways to enhance
educational opportunities" for students in the racially
unbalanced schools of the district. This plan was to give
minority students a wider choice of schools to attend and
provide "interracial educational experiences" short of
full-scale integration. Nyquist noted the "inexorable trend"
toward mostly segregated schools in the city and said this
trend could "only be reversed by factors over which the
school authorities have no control." He also stated that
"particular care must be taken in the development of an
integration plan to insure that efforts designed to achieve
greater integration in some schools do not destroy or
seriously impair the integration of other schools."

In its original appeal to the commissioner, the Board said
the district was steadily losing white families at a rate that
one Board official placed at about a thousand white
students a year. This was startlingly confirmed by the
following statistics: In 1976, four years after the Canarsie
school confrontation, JHS 285 in East Flatbush, had
dropped from 42 percent "Other" to 13 percent; JHS 211
from 70 percent "Other" to 58 percent; and JHS 68 from
98 percent "Other" to 64 percent.

To some, the Canarsie disaster was less "a test of the
school system's willingness to enforce integration" than,
in actuality, "a test of the limits of decentralization and of
the central board's willingness to assert its legal authority."
To others, the Board never had any unequivocal policy
upon which they might move toward racial or class

integration. Nor was it ever really clear how much or how little was wanted by many blacks. Certainly, their most prominent spokespersons did not agree. Nor was it really clear what the different white groups would permit. They were no more monolithic than nonwhites.

To some, the Canarsie decision was a mistake. "It was not integration. All it did was reinforce bigoted white attitudes by keeping a relatively few black kids out of some school."

Could anything have been done to prevent Canarsie? In a lengthy *New York Times* interview with Joseph Monserrat and Harvey Scribner on October 30, 1972, a questioner raised the issue.

Q: Could the whole Canarsie confrontation have been averted if the District 18 Community Board had assigned the Brownsville children to JHS 68 [Bildersee] before the opening of school?

Monserrat: Absolutely.

Scribner: No question about it.

What lessons, then, could one draw from Canarsie? What options are there for a city with a shrinking number of black and white youngsters in the middle-income range? Why are those children the first to run away from schools that threaten to "tip"? If whites can be condemned as racists for doing so, are blacks then equally guilty? And for how long can state legislatures allow their suburban school districts to build fences about their communities and refuse to assume any responsibility for what basically is a metropolitan dilemma?

Above all, to answer these questions, moral leadership is needed. During the Canarsie debacle there was only silence from City Hall, from many religious leaders, from all those from whom one might have expected direction

and—perhaps naively—even a suggestion of compromise
and reconciliation. Instead, schoolchildren became the
pawns of adults.

A continuing dilemma of desegregation policy that did
surface in the Canarsie dispute was busing. In a recent
school year, a survey taken by the National Civil Rights
Commission revealed that only 17 percent of the nation's
white population and 49 percent of the nation's black
population favored busing to achieve integration. Little
wonder that conservative politicians and some not-so-
conservative ones have sought to capitalize on the avowed
dislike of involuntary busing. But, if these politicans have
been responsible for more heat than light on the subject,
so have those who adamantly maintain—despite mounting
evidence to the contrary—that busing is necessarily the key
to better education for black people.

The fact is that many blacks support busing only as a
last resort, hoping to achieve better education for their
children when everything else has failed. In the midst of
Boston's ordeal, in October of 1974, when rioting was
rampant, a parent of a black child being bused into South
Boston spoke her mind to a reporter. She said:

> I think a lot of people really don't want busing—but you
> have to support something and I haven't got a better
> solution. The real issue is quality education. In the
> poorer communities you have dilapidated rundown
> schools, and people feel if white children came in, it
> would be a way of getting something done about it.
> Lots of folks saw this as a last resort.

Parents tend to be fearful when their children are bused
into an area that they perceive, rightly or wrongly, as one of
high crime and violence, or one where their children are
likely to encounter hostility. This was as true in 1904 as it

was in 1974. In 1904, the New York City Board of Education recommended the busing of fifteen hundred schoolchildren from overcrowded Lower East Side schools that were 95 percent Jewish to the underutilized schools of "Hell's Kitchen" on the West Side of Manhattan. These were both poor neighborhoods—inhabited largely by immigrants or the children of immigrants—one Jewish and the other Irish. But to the poor Jewish immigrants, "Hell's Kitchen" conjured up images of toughs and street gangs and violence and fear for their children. A protest meeting was called at a Lower East Side settlement house and two thousand, usually passive, but now irate and bitter parents turned out to protect the welfare of their children. Speakers complained of the dangers of crosstown busing, and the interference with their children's religious education. But they were most concerned with the safety of their children in what they deemed to be a hostile and anti-Jewish neighborhood.

Unfortunately, then as today, the pawns are the children of the poor—of whatever ethnic or racial background. As Bayard Rustin has stated, integration cannot be achieved peacefully if it exempts middle-class or affluent whites and comes at the expense of the white working people. Rustin's fears have been tragically borne out in the streets of Boston.

In what could become an important benchmark for future court decisions, Federal Judge Robert E. DeMascio of Detroit, in August 1975, rejected two desegregation proposals, each involving substantial amounts of busing for the Detroit school system. He ordered the Detroit school board to devise a less sweeping plan for achieving desegregation, involving less busing and an attempt to stabilize the neighborhoods of Detroit. He agreed with the contention of the board of education that desegregation could be legally accomplished through the elimination of "white identifiable schools" (schools having a white student

population exceeding 70 percent). Detroit's School Board
President Cornelius Golightly, who is himself black, called
the court's approach "very reasonable." Previously,
Coleman Young, Detroit's first black mayor, had filed a brief
before Judge DeMascio, contending that busing in Detroit
would "have the opposite effect of that desired—schools
will be resegregated instead of desegregated."

In June of 1976, the United States Supreme Court held,
in a 6 to 3 decision, that to prove a constitutional violation
of civil rights, plaintiffs must show that a law or other official
act has a "discriminatory purpose," as well as a
"discriminatory impact." The ruling was in *Washington* v.
Davis, a case involving two blacks whose applications to
become District of Columbia policemen had been rejected.
The two men challenged the constitutionality of a standard
government literacy test, because a higher percentage of
blacks than whites failed the test. This meant, they said, that
the test violated their rights to "due process." The Court,
in rejecting the challenge to the constitutionality of this
literacy test, noted that the two blacks "could no more
successfully claim that the test denied them equal
protection than could white applicants who also failed."

The Burger Court followed this principle on January 10,
1977, when it ruled, in a 5 to 3 decision, that the refusal of
the nearly all-white Chicago suburb of Arlington Heights to
change zoning restrictions, whose practical effect was to
block construction of racially integrated low- and moderate-
income housing, was not unconstitutional just because it
had a "racially disproportionate impact." To be
unconstitutional, the Court said, there must also be an
"intent" or a "purpose" to discriminate.

For several months after the 1976 *Davis* decision, many
observers wondered where the Court's emphasis on "intent"
would lead—especially in the area of school desegregation.
The Arlington Heights case was a signal of the Court's later

action in a case involving Indianapolis area schools. The Supreme Court sent the case back to a Federal Appeals Court, directing that court to give further consideration to the case in light of the high court's new emphasis in the two previously mentioned cases—*Washington* v. *Davis* and *Arlington Heights.* It held that discriminatory "intent," and not just discriminatory "effect," had to be proven in order to make a case of unconstitutional racial discrimination stick.

Many are now beginning to wonder whether these new decisions mean that the Supreme Court's thrust in the first Northern desegregation decision is delimited. In *Keyes,* the high court had announced that, "finding of intentionally segregative school board actions in a meaningful portion of a school system creates a presumption that other segregated schooling within the system is not adventitious." Some observers feel that the new emphasis on the doctrine of "intent" as against "effect" and not on mathematical racial formulas that some of the lower courts have used in the past could establish a new yardstick and thus a new climate of opinion in this area. Some look upon it negatively, suggesting that the Supreme Court—following a straight line from *Milliken* v. *Bradley* to *Arlington Heights* to *Indianapolis*—appears to be tightening the ring of white suburbs around the black core of most major American cities. Others look upon the new emphasis positively and see it as an indication of a breakthrough, a path away from the bruising racial "ratio" battle of the past that did not achieve enough for either black or white students to warrant its social cost in discord. They see it as a substantial move in the right direction.

Given the Supreme Court's recent decision in *Milliken,* if the lower courts continue to order involuntary busing to achieve racial balance, the suburbs will generally enhance their position as white sanctuaries sprinkled, to a limited degree, with members of the black middle class. Boston has already had a marked increase in its parochial school enrollment. Other cities under busing orders—for example, San Francisco, Norfolk, Washington, and Pasadena—will probably continue to experience the flight of large numbers of the middle class, both white and black. The long-term result could be further deterioration of the cities, increased racial tension, and urban school systems that are even less able to provide good education for those most in need of it.

But, even if the Detroit and Indianapolis cases had been decided differently, so as to encourage metropolitan desegregation programs, a reappraisal of present desegregation methods would, in the long run, have become inevitable. The deep-seated public resentment against involuntary busing, felt even by many of those who favor integration, suggests that, although extension of school desegregation plans to the suburbs would help to reduce flight from the cities, flight into private schools would probably accelerate and intensify. Furthermore, the events in Boston and Louisville are likely to be repeated elsewhere, and, however dedicated the courts may be to the concept of desegregation, they will be under increasing pressure to avoid issuing orders that can be implemented only by force.

The late Carl Becker once wrote, "The case for democracy is that it accepts the rational and humane values as ends and proposes as the means of realizing them the minimum of coercion and the maximum of voluntary assent." Unfortunately, the means used in attempting to foster desegregation have often maximized coercion and minimized voluntary assent, with sadly predictable consequences.

In view of the comparatively poor record of accomplishment in two decades of desegregation efforts and the questionable educational value of largely mechanical and inflexible court orders geared to numbers rather than to the needs of children, a frank reappraisal would have been made long ago were it not for the importance of desegregation as a symbol of social justice for black people. But reappraisal need not, and must not, diminish efforts to attain social justice. On the contrary, its purpose is to make desegregation efforts more effective by gearing them to changes that are educationally sound and realistically obtainable and that encourage cooperation rather than confrontation. Desegregation plans that ignore these factors actually make the achievement of integrated schooling more difficult, and bring us no closer to the goal of an integrated society.

Out of the debris of past failures, a new approach is gradually emerging. In Detroit, where the *Milliken* decision has forced the Court to face the realities of desegregating a predominantly minority school system, plans calling for extensive involuntary busing have been rejected or scaled down in an effort to encourage stability in rather than flight from the public schools. In Detroit and Atlanta with court approval, and in New York without legal proceedings, desegregation efforts are now concentrated on increasing minority representation in those schools having a predominantly white student population. In Boston, after two years of rioting, a series of "magnet schools" has been created, with programs attractive to both black and white students.

One might very well ask why these magnet schools were not planned, organized, and implemented before the rioting in Boston rather than after the senseless and tragic violence. In New York City, a magnet school (Mark Twain Junior High School), emphasizing the arts and geared to intellectually gifted children, was carefully organized in a year's time as the expression and fulfillment of a federal court's desegregation order. Its creation depolarized racial animosities, and it opened in the fall of 1975 with overwhelming community support—changing a school that was previously 20 percent "Other" to 70 percent "Other." Community stability has been enhanced not only by the opening of such a magnet school, but also by the procedure for placing children through a voluntary option. The selection process includes an objective examination as well as a thorough review of the student's record. Equally important to its successful implementation is the fact that the community school board actually developed the plan with a high degree of community involvement.

All busing to Mark Twain Junior High School is voluntary, and the school has a waiting list of children whose parents want them to be bused to a markedly superior educational institution, even though it is located in a high-crime area. These are many of the same parents who, a year earlier, threatened to boycott the school if their children, in the name of "desegregation," were removed from their neighborhood school and through "forced" busing made to attend what was then a markedly inferior school.

The future may yield other useful approaches. But, whatever the approach, we are coming to understand that successful integration requires far more than the physical movement of students. It requires an intensive human relations effort within the community. Ideally, stable, integrated schools should grow out of a total community effort encompassing housing, schools, economic development, and community service programs. But much can be accomplished short of this ideal so long as the importance of community support and participation is recognized. All too often, however, good community relations have been ignored as well-meaning judges, urged on by advocates of mathematical ratios, have issued sweeping desegregation orders.

Such orders ignore the profound fear parents have of losing the small voice they still have in their children's

schools. Working-class people—both black and white—
have a particularly strong fear of street violence entering
the corridors and classrooms of their children's schools.
They sense that many of today's schools are undergoing
major social and economic change, which they perceive as
resulting in a deterioration rather than an improvement in
the quality of education. The result is flight or bitter
resentment and hostility. Under such circumstances, the
real task—to translate desegregation into meaningful
integration—cannot even begin to be accomplished.

The courts in the future would do far better to seek
realistic levels of desegregation, concentrating less on
quantity and more on the quality of educational opportunity.
One such approach would involve a scaling down of
all-encompassing desegregation objectives to those
actually and readily attainable locally, while giving minority
students the option of either staying in improved and
perhaps specialized neighborhood schools or transferring
to predominantly nonminority schools. Another would be to
consider open housing in minimizing segregated schools.

This would represent a departure from some of the
massive busing decrees of the past, a change based upon a
recognition of new national educational priorities that
highlight children's needs, educational achievement, and
school-community stability. It would offer the possibility of
stable, nondiscriminatory school systems, in which the
prime emphasis and concern could come to be the
attainment of that difficult and most important goal of all
—a decent education for all of our children.

Conclusions

The progression from Ocean Hill–Brownsville to Canarsie is the movement from black community control to white community control. It is also the rejection by both communities of the notion of integration in the face of the imperatives of changing demographic conditions, and it represents the tensions inherent in ethnic assertiveness and ethnic assimilation.

To some observers, this period may stand out as a testament to the triumph of politics over education. Or to the misdirection of effort to the solution of ethnic rivalries over the more important problems of education.

An alternate interpretation is possible. As we considered a range of problems from community control to management reform, from educational change to student rights, the perspective constantly returned to concerns of ethnicity. Indeed, members of the Interim Board of Education spent most of their time trying to resolve social conflicts, which, for the most part, expressed themselves in terms of competition between the dominant white ethnic groups and new nonwhite ethnic groups.

At the bottom of the controversy was a subtle, but sometimes blatant numbers game. As the black and Hispanic student populations in parts of the city began increasing, white parents feared that schools in their neighborhoods would "tip." This meant that the white percentage would decrease sufficiently so that white flight would accelerate. Whether or not "tipping" is an accurate expression of social reality, it was certainly believed to be so by many and was given as the chief reason for white flight. Belief in this phenomenon made many white parents fight to keep nonwhite students out of their schools.

A second version of the numbers game was played by nonwhite parents. As their numbers increased, they began seeing a school system composed of nonwhite students and white teachers. These parents raised legitimate questions about the effects on their children of being raised in schools where whites were the role models and authority figures. This argument was made more cogent by the realization in the black and Hispanic communities that their numerical superiority could be used to impose new hiring imperatives on the school system. Opening up teaching and administrative jobs to their own group members was a powerful incentive to emphasizing the importance of nonwhite pedagogical staffs. The accompanying table indicates how the numbers have been changing for blacks over the last eight decades.

These numbers games indicated an underlying social conflict between the whites and the nonwhites, the former attempting to maintain their status and jobs, the latter attempting to achieve the same status and jobs. Ethnic politics was at bottom a social competition for the outputs of the social system. The older Anglo-Saxon group was aloof, but intervened from time to time through such media as the Ford Foundation and the Economic Development Council.

Are the blacks and Hispanics the last new ethnic groups to make their demands upon the educational system in large cities? Perhaps. Surely, though, ethnicity will not disappear. For ethnicity in the schools is a reflection of ethnicity in the larger society and the success of ethnic assertiveness as a strategy in attaining social mobility in American society.

For some, ethnic issues are merely a diversion in the eventual social confrontation between the haves and

BLACK PROPORTION OF GENERAL POPULATION, ELEMENTARY AND SECONDARY SCHOOL ENROLLMENT, AND ELEMENTARY AND SECONDARY TEACHERS IN 16 CITIES, 1890–1970

City	1890	1900	1910	1920	1930	1940	1950	1960	1970
Baltimore									
General population	15.4	15.6	15.2	14.8	17.7	19.3	23.7	34.7	46.4
School enrollment	12.0	12.9	12.9	12.2	15.7	21.4	27.6	41.3	58.0
Teachers	1.3	8.3	M.D.	12.4	16.7	19.0	M.D.	M.D.	45.4
Boston									
General population	1.8	2.1	2.0	2.2	2.6	3.1	5.0	9.1	16.3
School enrollment	1.4	1.3	1.4	1.5	2.2	3.0	M.D.	11.7	23.0
Teachers	.1	.4	.3	.5	.8	.5	M.D.	M.D.	5.8
Chicago									
General population	1.3	1.8	2.0	4.1	6.9	8.2	13.6	22.9	32.7
School enrollment	.8	1.1	1.2	2.7	5.3	8.8	15.4	28.5	43.7
Teachers	M.D.	.7	.6	1.2	2.3	M.D.	M.D.	M.D.	26.5
Cleveland									
General population	1.1	1.6	1.5	4.3	8.0	9.6	16.2	28.6	38.3
School enrollment	.8	1.1	1.0	2.9	6.4	11.1	18.8	33.7	48.1
Teachers	.6	.4	M.D.	1.8	1.9	3.1	M.D.	M.D.	38.9
Dallas									
General population	21.0	21.2	19.6	15.1	14.9	17.1	13.1	19.0	24.9
School enrollment	18.2	19.3	16.3	14.0	13.0	17.8	13.3	19.7	30.8
Teachers	15.1	M.D.	M.D.	13.8	13.6	16.1	M.D.	M.D.	22.3

Detroit

General population	1.7	1.4	1.2	4.1	7.7	9.2	16.2	28.9	43.7
School enrollment	1.4	1.1	.9	2.8	6.1	9.1	16.7	33.8	53.1
Teachers	M.D.	.7	M.D.	.8	1.1	1.6	M.D.	M.D.	38.5

Houston

General population	37.6	32.7	30.4	24.6	21.7	22.4	20.9	22.9	25.7
School enrollment	36.0	28.3	29.1	23.5	19.9	22.2	21.0	23.6	29.2
Teachers	34.4	M.D.	M.D.	24.8	20.9	22.5	M.D.	M.D.	26.6

Indianapolis

General population	8.7	9.4	9.3	11.0	12.1	13.2	15.0	20.6	18.0
School enrollment	8.3	9.2	5.5	10.9	12.3	14.4	17.3	23.3	20.9
Teachers	4.5	5.8	6.7	9.1	11.2	12.4	M.D.	M.D.	14.9

Los Angeles

General population	2.5	2.1	2.4	2.7	3.1	4.2	8.7	13.5	17.9
School enrollment	2.5	2.0	2.4	3.0	3.2	4.4	11.3	18.6	22.2
Teachers	M.D.	0	M.D.	.6	.6	.9	M.D.	M.D.	14.3

Milwaukee

General population	.2	.3	.3	.5	1.3	1.5	3.4	8.4	14.7
School enrollment	.1	.2	.1	.3	1.1	1.5	M.D.	11.1	20.8
Teachers	M.D.	.2	M.D.	0	.1	.1	M.D.	M.D.	9.7

BLACK PROPORTION OF GENERAL POPULATION, SCHOOL ENROLLMENT, AND TEACHERS IN 16 CITIES, 1890-1970 (CONTINUED)

City	1890	1900	1910	1920	1930	1940	1950	1960	1970
New Orleans									
General population	26.6	27.1	26.3	26.1	28.3	30.1	31.9	37.2	45.0
School enrollment	22.5	22.4	21.1	24.6	27.1	32.0	38.3	43.2	55.3
Teachers	6.2	15.9	M.D.	14.0	20.4	20.7	M.D.	M.D.	42.5
New York									
General population	M.D.	1.8	1.9	2.7	4.7	6.1	9.5	14.0	21.1
School enrollment	M.D.	1.1	1.1	1.6	3.5	6.4	10.4	17.0	28.2
Teachers	M.D.	.8	.4	.6	1.3	1.2	M.D.	M.D.	8.2
Philadelphia									
General population	3.8	4.8	5.5	7.4	11.3	13.0	18.2	26.4	33.6
School enrollment	3.2	3.3	3.9	5.6	9.7	14.5	20.8	31.4	42.1
Teachers	1.0	2.4	2.2	3.0	4.5	4.1	M.D.	M.D.	24.1
San Antonio									
General population	12.5	14.1	11.1	8.9	7.8	7.6	7.0	7.1	7.6
School enrollment	13.0	13.2	9.5	8.5	7.5	6.5	M.D.	7.1	7.9
Teachers	15.8	10.9	M.D.	6.8	9.0	7.5	M.D.	M.D.	9.1
San Francisco									
General population	.6	.5	.4	.5	.6	.8	5.6	10.0	13.4
School enrollment	1.4	.4	.2	.3	.4	.6	12.9	26.8	21.8
Teachers	M.D.	.1	M.D.	.1	0	.1	M.D.	M.D.	7.7

St. Louis

General population	5.9	6.2	6.4	9.0	11.4	13.3	17.9	28.6	40.9
School enrollment	4.8	5.0	4.8	7.8	10.5	14.4	22.5	37.5	53.8
Teachers	8.3	5.6	5.7	7.4	11.1	12.4	M.D.	M.D.	41.7

NOTE: "M.D." indicates
missing data

The data were taken from The United States Census Bureau:
Census of Populations, 1890–1970.

have-nots. To some, ethnicity is merely a stalking-horse for class division. For three observers and participants, however, ethnicity has been much more: a pervasive fact of life during our tenure on the Board.

Recently the New York City Board of Education has fallen on hard times and is critically reviewed for its inefficiency and corruption. But, in truth, inefficiency and corruption had been small issues compared to the need for resolving the ethnic conflicts beleaguering the school system. And, in that arena, the Interim Board of Education excelled.

The Interim Board of Education was performing its prescribed role as an intermediary between the educational bureaucracy and outside forces. It responded well and adroitly. For some, too adroitly—for example, in eventually eliminating the demonstration districts without major mishap.

Boards of education in Chicago, Detroit, Los Angeles, Washington, D.C., and elsewhere were similarly concerned. But what of educational issues like open classrooms, new media techniques, team teaching? Those issues received attention, though not much from the top, reflecting the fact that the outside world was not very concerned about them.

Throughout our tenure at the New York City Board of Education, there were those who said, "When will the Board of Education be concerned about quality education, rather than the politics of accommodation?" And yet, as the Board of Education moved toward each educational issue, the underlying social and ethnic conflict returned. In the end, it became clear to us that mediating social conflict between the new, rising, nonwhite ethnics and the dominant white ethnics was the main job of the Board of Education. And it looks to us as if other big city boards of education were similarly occupied. In the only other in-depth study of a big city educational system, Paul Petersen, in *School Politics Chicago Style,* focused on decentralization, teacher power, and desegregation as the major issues confronting the Chicago school system.

Shouldn't a board of education be concerned with upgrading education? Perhaps. As the educational process now stands—and decentralization and community control did nothing to change that—it depends upon students interacting in a classroom with a teacher who is trained in a school of education, which is part of a national network and uses materials designed by national publishers.

Any strategy to change teaching must concentrate on the classroom teacher, or depart radically from the current operation of the educational system through the country. And any departure must fly in the face of the nationally organized union power of today's classroom teachers. Much more than we realize, teaching techniques are developed, disseminated, and controlled by these national institutions.

Boards of education or other forms of school governance in individual cities can make some breakthroughs and improve teaching to a limited degree. But they are weak when compared to the national institutions currently dominating the educational scene.

Perhaps the times have changed and new needs have arisen for leadership at the top. Perhaps we need to redefine the place of classrooms and teachers in a world dominated by the mass media. Boards of education are neither well equipped nor inclined to confront these issues.

To us it looks as if the ethnic influence on education may lessen if the ethnic dimension of local politics throughout the country decreases. Boards of education will have little more effect on educational technique than they have had in the past. Education will continue to be more a badge of social status than a lever for equalizing opportunity in the social system.

If these prospects seem conservative to many, so be it.

For, in our experience, the educational system is essentially
a conservative institution, unusually sensitive to the
demands of emergent ethnic groups, but still a captive of the
power realities of the larger society.

Selected Bibliography

Altshuler, Alan. *Community Control*. New York: Pegasus, 1970.

Bundy, McGeorge et al. *Reconnection for Learning: A Community School System for New York City*. New York: Praeger, 1969.

Callahan, Raymond. *The Cult of Efficiency*. Chicago: University of Chicago Press, 1962.

Carmichael, Stokley, and Hamilton, Charles V. *Black Power: The Politics of Liberation in America*. New York: Random House, 1967.

Crain, Robert L. *The Politics of School Desegregation*. Chicago: Aldine, 1968.

Cremin, Lawrence. *Public Education*. New York: Basic Books, 1977.

Cronin, Joseph M. *The Control of Urban Schools: Perspectives on the Power of Educational Reformers*. New York: Free Press, 1973.

Donovan, John. *The Politics of Poverty*. New York: Bobbs-Merrill, 1967; 2nd ed., 1973.

Drucker, Peter F. *The Practice of Management*. New York: Harper & Row, 1954.

Fein, Leonard. *The Ecology of the Public Schools: An Inquiry into Community Control*. New York: Praeger, 1971.

Gittell, Marilyn et al. *School Boards and School Policy*. New York: Praeger, 1973.

Glazer, Nathan, and Moynihan, Daniel. *Beyond the Melting Pot*. Cambridge, Mass.: MIT Press, 1963; 2nd ed. 1970.

Harrison, Bennett. *Education Training and the Urban Ghetto*. Baltimore: Johns Hopkins University Press, 1972.

159

Hartley, Harry. *Educational Planning-Programming-Budgeting.* Englewood Cliffs, N.J.: Prentice Hall, 1968.

Hendrick, Irving G., and Jones, Reginald L. *Student Dissent in the Schools.* Boston: Houghton Mifflin, 1970.

Herrick, Mary. *The Chicago Schools: A Social and Political History.* Beverly Hills, Cal.: Sage Publications, 1971.

Immegart, Glenn, and Pilecki, Francis. *An Introduction to Systems for the Educational Administrator.* Reading, Mass.: Addison-Wesley, 1973.

Katz, Michael B. *Class, Bureaucracy and Schools: The Illusion of Educational Change in America.* New York: Praeger, 1971.

Kirst, Michael W. *The Politics of Education.* Berkeley: McCutchen, 1970.

Kluger, Richard. *Simple Justice.* New York: Knopf, 1976.

Knezevich, Stephen. *Administration of Public Education.* New York: Harper & Row, 1962, 1969.

Knezevich, Stephen. *Program Budgeting (PPBS).* Berkeley, Cal.: McCutchen, 1973.

La Noue, George, and Smith, Bruce. *The Politics of School Decentralization.* Lexington, Mass.: D. C. Heath, 1973.

Lieberson, Stanley. *Ethnic Patterns in American Cities.* New York: Free Press, 1963.

Litt, Edgar. *Ethnic Politics in America.* New York: Scott, Foresman, 1970.

Lowi, Theodore. *At the Pleasure of the Mayor.* New York: Free Press, 1964.

McGregor, Douglas. *The Human Side of Enterprise.* New York: McGraw-Hill, 1960.

Minter, Thomas. *Intermediate School 201, Manhattan Center of Controversy.* Cambridge, Mass.: Harvard University, Graduate School of Education, 1967.

Mort, Paul. *Educational Adaptability.* New York: Metropolitan School Study Council, undated.

Ornstein, Allan. *Metropolitan Schools: Administrative Decentralization vs. Community Control.* Metuchen, N.J.: Scarecrow Press, 1974.

Patterson, Ernest. *Black City Politics.* New York: Dodd, Mead, 1974.

Peterson, Paul. *School Politics Chicago Style.* Chicago: University of Chicago Press, 1976.

Ravitch, Diane. *The Great School Wars, New York City, 1805–1973.* New York: Basic Books, 1974.

Resnik, Henry S. *Turning on the System.* New York: Pantheon, 1970.

Ross, Arthur, and Hill, Herbert. *Employment, Race and Poverty.* New York: Harcourt, Brace & World, Harbinger, 1967.

Schrag, Peter. *Village School Downtown.* Boston: Beacon Press, 1967.

St. John, Nancy. *School Desegregation: Outcomes for Children.* New York: John Wiley & Sons, 1975.

Sullivan, Neil V., and Stewart, Evelyn S. *Now Is the Time: Integration in the Berkeley Schools.* Bloomington: Indiana University Press, 1969.

Tyack, David B. *The One Best System.* Cambridge, Mass.: Harvard University Press, 1974.

United States Immigration Commission. *Children of Immigrants.* Washington, D.C.: U.S. Government.

Wilson, James Q. *Negro Politics.* Glencoe, Ill.: Free Press, 1960.

Index

Adams-Morgan School, 51
Afro-American Students Association, 97, 104
Alternative schools, 67–72, 79–89
American Association of School Administrators, 55
American Federation of Teachers (AFT), 2, 47, 49, 101
American Magazine, 45
American School Board Journal, 110
Anderson, James, 47
Anglo-Saxons, 7, 11, 123, 151
Anker, Irving, 61, 132–34, 139
Anti-Defamation League of B'nai B'rith, 129
Antiwar movement, 90, 111, 116
Arlington Heights case, 144–45
Arricale, Frank, 61, 62
Atlanta, 124–26, 147
Atlantic Plaza Towers, 17, 23
Attendance, school, 72, 84–85
At the Pleasure of the Mayor, 7
Austin High School, 113–14

Badillo, Herman, 13, 75
Baltimore, 53, 113, 152
Bard, Bernard, 91
Becker, Carl, 146
Bedford-Stuyvesant, 6, 34, 37
Bell, Griffin, 125
Bergtraum, Murry, 13, 19, 29, 92, 101, 105
Beyond the Melting Pot, 7
Bilingualism, 44
Black culture, 4–5, 95, 113
Blacks, 1–6, 10–12, 46, 51, 62, 83, 87, 150–51
  in Canarsie case study, 126–49
  in Ocean Hill-Brownsville, 16–39
  as proportion of general population, 152–55
  school integration and, 117–26, 143–49
  student rights and, 90–91, 95–107, 112–14
Blockbusting, 131
Boston, 14, 40, 142–43, 147, 152
Bowker, Albert, 78

Boycott, school, 133–37, 148
Brewster, Kingman, 75
Bronx Park Community Project, 51
Brooklyn Diocese (Catholic), 32
Brooklyn Technical High School, 96
Brown, Nathan, 94–95, 103
Brown case, 117–19
Brownsville, 126, 129–31; *see also* Ocean Hill-Brownsville
Brydges, Earl, 30
Bunche, Ralph, 75
Bundy, McGeorge, 25–26, 74
Bundy report, 26, 32
Bureaucracy, educational, 40–65
  decentralization and, 50–52
  EDC and, 57–62
  establishing system of, 42–46
  management reform of, 52–57, 64
  teacher unionism and, 47–50
Bureaucracy in Education, 47
Business, 43, 45
Busing, 32, 119, 126, 142–49

California, 12, 38, 53, 55, 94, 107, 113, 124
Callahan, Raymond, 46, 56
Campbell, Leslie, 20, 22–23, 33, 36
Canarsie, 1, 14, 38
  case study of, 126–49
Canarsie High School, 98
Career education, 82–84
Carnegie Foundation, 67
Carter, Jimmy, 49
Catholic Teachers Association, 29
Center for Research and Education in American Liberties, 111
Champion, George, 57, 60
Chicago, 40, 42, 52, 53, 55, 62, 90, 113, 124, 144, 152
Chicanos, 123
Chisholm, Shirley, 29, 30–31, 36–37
Cincinnati, 55
City as School, 83, 86
Civil Rights Act (1964), 110, 118
Civil rights movement, 90, 111, 116
Clark, Kenneth B., 35, 74
Clark, Ramsey, 75
Clark County (Nevada), 53

Cleaver, Eldridge, 97
Cloward, Richard, 3, 38
Cohen, Wilbur, 75
Collective bargaining, 48
Community control
  background of, 1–15
  in Canarsie, 38, 126–42
  conclusions about, 150
  in Ocean Hill-Brownsville, 16–39
  as a strategy, 38–39
Community School Board, 18, 127, 131–35
Compensatory education, 74
Connor, Robert, 13
Constitutional rights, 109–15
Corporal punishment, 115–16
Crim, Alonzo A., 126
Crisis in the Classroom, 67
Critical Path Method, 52, 56
Critics, school, 66–73
Cult of Efficiency, 46
Curricular changes, 95, 113

Dade County (Florida) Public Schools, 53
Dallas, 40, 42, 55, 62, 67, 113, 152
Dearborn Heights School District, 124
DeCecco, John F., 111
Decentralization legislation, 12–13, 21, 27
  failures of, 38–39
  school bureaucracy and, 50–52
  school reform and, 74–88
  see also Canarsie, Ocean Hill-Brownsville
DeMascio, Robert E., 143–44
Democratic party, 5, 19, 21, 75
Demonstration school districts, 17–18, 29
Demonstrations, student, 94, 105–6, 107, 111, 112–14
Desegregation cases, school, 119–22; see also Integration, school
Detroit, 11, 12, 38, 40, 51, 55, 64, 124, 143–44, 146–47, 153
Dewey, John, 69
Disruption, acts of, 94–95
Donovan, Bernard, 17–18, 94–95, 101
Douglas County (Colorado), 53
Drucker, Peter F., 54, 57

East Flatbush, 128–38
Ebbets Field School, 83

Economic Development Council (EDC), 41, 57–62, 151
"Economic Measure of School Efficiency, An," 45
Edison, Mike, 36
Education, Training and the Urban Ghetto, 7
Efficiency bureaus, 46
Elementary and Secondary Education Act (1965), 10–11, 139
Estes, Noland, 42, 55, 62
Ethnic groups, 7–10, 44–45, 62, 69, 88, 123
  new, 2, 7, 10–12, 46, 50, 51, 62, 151–52
Experimental schools, 67–72, 79–89

Feldman, Sam, 108
Feulner, Helen Donovan, 62
"15 Demands," 95–98, 105
Financial Accounting, 53
Flag salute, 109–10
Ford Foundation, 12, 25–26, 32, 38, 53, 78–80, 83, 84, 151

Gaines, Edythe, 61
Galbraith, John Kenneth, 75
Germans, 103, 123
Gifford, Bernard, 61, 62
Gittell, Marilyn, 38
Glasser, Ira, 27
Glazer, Nathan, 7, 9
Goldberg, Arthur, 75
Golightly, Cornelius, 144
Goodman, Paul, 66, 69
Green v. County School Board of New Kent County (1968), 120
Griffiths, Daniel, 75–76

Haaren High School, 83–86
Harlem, 3, 12, 26, 37
Harlem Parents Council, 3
Harlem Prep, 81
Harris, Louis, 35, 36
Harrison, Bennett, 7
Harrison High School, 113
Hartley, Harry, 53
Hawley, Amos, 3
Hayes, Frederick O'Reilly, 75–76
Helmsley, Harry, 58
Higher Horizons, 73
High School Students Rights Coalition, 104
High School Teachers Association of New York City, 46
High schools, alternative, 80–85

Hispanics, 1–6, 10–12, 46, 51, 62, 83, 124, 150–51
  in Ocean Hill-Brownsville, 16–39
  student rights and, 90–91
  see also Puerto Ricans
Holt, John, 66
Hughes, Richard J., 68

Illich, Ivan, 66
Illinois, 53
Immigrants, 44, 143
"Independent Study Model," 86
Indianapolis, 145–46, 153
Inkester School District, 124
Integration, school, 117–26, 143–49
Interim Board of Education for the City of New York (1969), 13, 18–20, 27
Intermediate School 201 (NYC), 3, 12, 26, 33, 37
Irish Catholics, 7–9, 11, 62, 103, 123
Italians, 7, 8, 11, 16, 32, 62, 87, 98, 103, 123

Jackson, Maynard, 125
Jefferson High School, 107
Jews, 1–2, 8, 11, 16, 62, 87, 98, 123, 129, 143
Jobs, 6, 10, 82–83, 88, 103
John Adams High School, 68
John Bowne High School, 102
John Dewey High School, 67–68
Johnson, Lyndon B., 10, 53, 118
Julia Richmond High School, 102
Junior High School 68 (NYC), 127, 134–40
Junior High School 211 (NYC), 127, 134–40
Junior High School 271 (NYC), 20, 22–23
Junior High School 285 (NYC), 127–37

Kelly, Colin, 128
Kennedy, John F., 48
Keyes et al. v. School District No. 1, Denver, Colorado, et al. (1973), 121, 145
King, Lonnie, Jr., 125
Kohl, Herbert, 66
Kozol, Jonathan, 66, 69

Lachman, Seymour, 13, 18, 20–24, 27–35, 96–97, 101
La Guardia, Fiorello, 8
Lake View High School, 114

Lavinsky, Larry, 117n
Learning Cooperative, 79–80
Lelyveld, Joseph, 87
Leonard, George, 66, 69
Levine, Abe, 105
Leviss, Sidney, 13
Levy, Gustave, 58
Lewis, Blanche, 78
Lieberson, Stanley, 6
Lindsay, John, vii, 1–2, 18, 25, 26, 31, 36, 75, 87, 94, 136
Los Angeles, 11, 12, 40, 51, 52, 53, 55, 107, 124, 153
Los Angeles Times, 107
Lotz, John, 75
Low, Seth, 8
Lower East Side (NYC), 12, 26, 38, 143
Lowi, Theodore, 7–8
Luce, Charles, 58

McCoy, Rhody, 1–2, 17, 20–24, 28–29, 31, 33, 34–37
McGregor, Douglas, 54
Machines, political, 8–9
McNamara, Robert, 53, 75
Magnet schools, 147–48
Management by Objectives (MBO), 52, 54–56, 64
Management Information Systems (MIS), 52, 64
Management reforms, 52–57, 64
Mark Twain Junior High School, 147–48
Mathews, Alfredo, Jr., 61
Matthews, Marjorie, 34
Mayer, Martin, 72
Meade, Mary E., 13, 19, 100, 106
Memphis, 53
Mena (Arkansas) case, 110–11
Metropolitan Applied Research Center, 35
Mexican-Americans, 107, 112–13
Meyer Levin School, 128–29
Meyers, Jerome, 7
Miami, 55, 115
Michigan, 12, 38
Miller, Wilbert, 127
Milliken v. Bradley, 121, 145, 147
Milwaukee, 53, 153
Mishler, Jacob, 139
Mitchel, John, 8
Monserrat, Joseph, 13, 19, 29–30, 31, 34, 101, 141
More Effective Schools, 73–74
Mort, Paul, 50

Motley, Constance Baker, 114–15
Moynihan, Daniel P., 7, 9

National Academy for School Ex-
    ecutives, 53
National Association for the Ad-
    vancement of Colored People
    (NAACP), 125
National Education Association
    (NEA), 46, 47, 49, 101
Native-American Protestants, 7–8,
    44, 62–63
New Haven, 7
New Jersey Street Academies, 68
Newsweek, 85
New York Board of Rabbis, 32
New York City, passim
    Board of Education, 24–26, 40–
        41, 57, 74–88, 91–101, 156–57
    Canarsie case study, 126–49
    decentralization plans, 51
    EDC survey in, 57–62
    ethnic conflicts and community
        control in, 1–15
    Human Resources Administra-
        tion, 82
    Interim Board of Education, 13,
        18–20, 27
    Ocean Hill-Brownsville, 16–39
    Planning Commission, 82
    proportion of blacks in general
        population in, 154
    school reform, 52–54, 73–89
    student rights in, 91–101
    teacher unionism in, 47–50
    Urban Coalition, 83–84
New York Civil Liberties Union, 27,
    104
New York Post, 91
New York State Board of Regents,
    136
New York State Education Depart-
    ment, 41
New York Times, 28, 41, 78, 85, 87,
    118, 125, 141
New York University, 53
North, the, 118–26
North Carolina Advancement School,
    70–71
Nyquist, Ewald B., 67, 78–79, 136,
    139–40

O'Brien, Larry, 75
Ocean Hill-Brownsville, 1, 12, 16–
    39, 51, 130
Oliver, C. Herbert, 20–23, 34, 36, 37

Open enrollment, 32, 95
Open housing, 149
Operations Research, 52

Parkway School, 67, 70, 83
Party machine, 8–9
Patten, Simon, 45
Pearl, Arthur, 72–73
Performance Planning, 54–56
Petersen, Paul, 156
Petrie, Don, 75
Philadelphia, 40, 53, 67, 69–72, 90,
    113, 124, 154
Pilgrim, Charles, 87
Pittsburgh, 55
Plan for the Revitalization of Local
    School Boards, 24
Planning, Programming, Budgeting
    Systems (PPBS), 52–54, 56, 64
Polatnick, Samuel, 62
Polner, Murray, 27, 36
Potts, Robert, 91
Powell, Adam Clayton, 5
Powell, Lewis F., Jr., 115
Press, student, 108
Principals, high school, 47, 91–93,
    95, 102
Program Evaluation and Review
    Technique (PERT), 56
Project Management, 52
Property, destruction of school, 94
Protestant churches, 32
Public Education Association, 80
Puerto Ricans, 1, 10, 16, 19, 25, 30,
    33, 36, 87, 96, 123, 129

Quotas, 7

Rand Corporation, 52
Reading failures, 72
"Reconnection to Learning," 80
Redfern, George, 55
Redmond, James, 62
Reeves, Donald, 104
Reform movements, 9–10, 42, 46,
    52–57, 64, 66–89
Regan, James, 19
Research Corporation of the As-
    sociation of School Business
    Officials, 53
Resnick, Harry, 70–71
Riverdale Research, 52
Robinson, Isaiah, 13, 19, 27, 33,
    100, 104, 106
Rosenthal, Alan, 48
Rustin, Bayard, 78, 143

St. Louis, 11, 12, 40, 155
Samuel Tilden High School, 131
San Francisco, 55, 67, 154
Sarnoff, Robert, 58
Satellite academies, 82–83
"School of Municipal Affairs," 86
School Politics Chicago Style, 156
School systems, big city, 42–46, 66–89
Scotch-Irish, 8
Scribner, Harvey B., vii, 22, 40–41, 48–49, 57–58, 60, 62–63, 67, 75–88, 127, 132, 133, 135–37, 141
Shanker, Albert, 1–2, 29, 30, 48–49, 75, 78, 102, 136
Shedd, Mark, 67, 69–72
Shriver, Sargent, 75
Silberman, Charles, 67
Slavs, 123
Sophia House, 81
South, the, 118–26
South Dakota, 112
Soviet Union, 126
Stanford Research Institute, 52
Stark, Abe, 13, 18
"Statement of Student Rights and Responsibilities," 108–9
Steingut, Stanley, 28, 29
Stewart, Waldaba, 99
Strike, teachers', 17–18
Student rights, 14, 90–116
Student Rights Mobilization, 104, 106
Stuyvesant High School, 114
Suburbs, 145–46
Sullivan, Neil, 75–76
Suspensions, student, 94, 95, 97, 110
Sutton, Percy, 13
Sviridoff, Mitchell, 35
Swann v. Charlotte-Mecklenberg Board of Education (1971), 120
Swanson, Bert, 36

Task Force on High School Redesign, 86
Taylor, Frederick W., 43, 45, 60
Teachers, 17–18, 47–50, 56
Tilden Houses, 126–38
Tinker v. Des Moines Independent Community School District, 109–10

"Tipping," 150–51
"Toward the 21st Century," 86
Tractman v. Anker, 115
Turning on the System: War in the Philadelphia Public Schools, 70
Tweed, William Marcy (Boss), 8
Two Bridges School District, 12, 26, 37–38

Unionism, teacher, 47–50, 56
United Federation of Teachers (UFT), 2, 75
United Parents Associations (UPA), 78, 87, 104
U.S. Department of Defense, 52–53
U.S. Department of Health, Education, and Welfare, 113
U.S. Office of Education, 53
U.S. Senate Immigration Commission, 44
U.S. Supreme Court, 109–15, 118–22, 144–45, 147
Urban Task Force, 29

Vann, Albert, 20, 23, 36
Vietnam War, 109, 111
Village School, 68
Vocational schools, 103

Wagner, Robert F., 25, 48
Wallace, George, 108
War on Poverty, 10
Washington, D.C., 11, 12, 38, 40, 51, 123–24
Washington v. Davis, 144–45
Weber, Max, 70
Weinstein, Jack, 75
Westin, Alan F., 111
Wicker, Tom, 118
Wilcox, Preston, 3
Working class, 143, 149
Wright, Sam, 21–22, 27–33, 36, 37, 132
Wriston, Walter, 75

Ylvisaker, Paul, 75
Young, Coleman, 144
Young Americans for Freedom, 103

Zimmer, Jack, 127, 131–35
Zoning, 126, 129